The Teachers' ... Toolkit

A companion website to accompany this book is available online
at: http://education.pollmullersercombe.continuumbooks.com

Please visit the link and register with us to receive your
password and access these downloadable resources.

If you experience any problems accessing the resources,
please contact Continuum at: info@continuumbooks.com

Also available from Continuum

100 Ideas for Teaching Design and Technology, David Spendlove

The Art and Design Teacher's Handbook, Susie Hodge

Pimp your Lesson!, Isabella Wallace and Leah Kirkman

The Teachers' Animation Toolkit

Britta Pollmüller and Martin Sercombe

continuum

Continuum International Publishing Group

The Tower Building
11 York Road
London SE1 7NX

80 Maiden Lane
Suite 704, New York
NY 10038

www.continuumbooks.com

British Library Cataloguing-in-Publication Data
A catalogue record for this book is available from the British Library.

ISBN: 978-1-4411-4525-3 (paperback)

Library of Congress Cataloging-in-Publication Data
Pollmüller, Britta.
The teachers' animation toolkit / Britta Pollmüller and Martin Sercombe.
    p. cm.
  ISBN 978-1-4411-4525-3–ISBN 978-1-4411-4796-7–
  ISBN 978-1-4411-3107-2   1. Animated films–Study and teaching (Secondary) 2. Animation (Cinematography)–Study and teaching (Secondary) I. Sercombe, Martin. II. Title.

  NC1765.P59 2011
  791.43—34–dc22   2010053756

Typeset by Newgen Imaging Systems Pvt Ltd, Chennai, India
Printed and bound in India

Note
All prices listed in this book were correct at the time of going to press but may be subject to change.

CONTENTS

Additional Contributions

James Clarke

Creative Practitioners

(supporting workshop delivery)
Britta Pollmüller
Karina Williams
Jonathan Lambert
Martin Sercombe

Original Research Funded by

NESTA
ESCalate
Norwich University College of the Arts
In association with Creative Partnerships

With special thanks to
Participating Schools

Dowson First School, Antingham First School,
Woodland View Middle School
Sprowston Middle School, Sprowston High School,
Broadland High School
Notre Dame High School, Heatherset High School,
Reepham High School

Participating Organizations

Open University and Schome Park,
ShortFuze (Moviestorm)
Reallusion (CrazyTalk)
Media Box, First Light Movies

Special thanks also go to

Simon Willmoth, Michael Spencer, Will Pearson, Rebecca Staples
Laura Budds, Mark Cotter, Julian Frank, David Arthur, Karen Bygrave
Sally Hirst, Caroline Denyer, Harriet Halstead, Hannah Giffard
James Durran, Margaret Quigley

INTRODUCTION

animation (n): the art of making inanimate objects appear to move. (Encyclopedia Britannica)

WHAT IS THE TEACHERS' ANIMATION TOOLKIT?

The Teachers' Animation Toolkit grew out of a 3-year research project which tested and evaluated ways to integrate animation into the school curriculum. This research identified the extremely valuable part animation can play in enhancing literacy and numeracy skills, and visual creativity among pupils of all ages. It also sought to identify the types of practical and theoretical support teachers urgently need to teach animation effectively.

This toolkit places creativity, risk-taking and imaginative play at the core of the learning experiences it seeks to support. As our culture becomes increasingly focused on a wide range of screen media (television, cinema, online content, computer games and mobile phones etc.) the time is right to engage with the creative potentials of these new formats.

Even Liam stood in front of me jumping up and down with the excitement of doing animation next year!! He has never been excited about anything he does in school.

(Rebecca Staples, Head of English)

The initial research for the toolkit targeted secondary education. However, many of the practical ideas assembled here can be adapted to suit primary age pupils, or 16- to 19-year-olds studying animation on A level or further education courses. The toolkit aims to show how 2D and 3D animation can form an important part of many subjects, including the Art and Design, English, PHSE, Citizenship, Photography and Media curricula. The processes involved in creating an animation project use skills and understandings such as: creative writing, team working, measuring, planning, organizing and developing awareness of the wider world. All of these skills and experiences can be readily assessed.

From the outset, we wanted the practice of animation to be explored alongside the teaching of media or cineliteracy. The toolkit aims to show teachers how the viewing of animated films can be a valuable starting point for classroom discussions around cineliteracy and can also be used as a theoretical frame of reference for the projects that they produce.

Animation is the most dynamic form of expression available to creative people . . . Animation is used in science, architecture, healthcare and broadcast journalism . . . it is simply everywhere!

(Paul Wells, *The Fundamentals of Animation*, Thames and Hudson 2006)

RESEARCH TECHNIQUES

Ten schools across Norfolk, UK took part in the research, which ran over a 3-year period between 2004 and 2007. It involved testing a wide variety of teaching approaches and animation genres then collecting evidence to evaluate their efficacy and the learning that had taken place. Evidence took the form of student sketchbooks, interviews, photographs and examples of student-made animations. Video recordings of lessons were made and handheld cameras were used to pick up on relevant issues, raised in discussions between practitioner and pupils or practitioner and teacher.

Pupils were asked to explain, in open discussion, their thought processes, their decision making and their overall responses to the assignment via the camera and evaluation sheets. These discussions were used to explore how pupils articulated the visual and text-based language of music, sound production and moving images. Their responses were complemented by after-class interviews with the teachers. The evidence was then edited in order to highlight key points and recommendations and prioritize the best practice for inclusion in this toolkit.

Teachers were provided with worksheets, showing how to animate without expensive technology and useful tips on what animations might be shown to the class. The worksheets promoting cineliteracy were carefully designed to fit within the UK curriculum standards. Many offered active learning, extension work and differentiated activities to suit all learners and to fit within 50/60 minutes of classroom time. Schemes of work focused on more advanced projects and took place over a series of lessons. All these materials were refined in response to teacher and student evaluation before being included in the toolkit.

Not only have you brought life into the department and demonstrated what amazing results can be achieved by our pupils, you have encouraged and inspired pupils who find the academic subjects more challenging. I have noticed some real positive changes in a particular group of challenging boys, who have really taken to the workshops . . . (One of these) rarely shows enthusiasm and is one of these 'too cool for school' types. I thought he would struggle with collaborative work and probably moan through the whole thing but he remained quiet and took part with little distraction. It was after the workshop when he went out of his way to find me to explain how much he loved the day and how he wanted to do more of this in the future.

(Dan Coombes, Head of Art, Flegg High School)

WHY USE ANIMATION IN THE CLASSROOM?

Animation is highly cross-curricular. It draws on a wide range of skills that can enhance the teaching of many different subjects.

In **English**, students' knowledge of film and television genres, narrative structure and character development can improve their abilities as readers and writers.

The study of animation history can support many of the key concepts that underpin the study of chronological, cultural and event-based **history**. An understanding of people and places can be gained through a study of animation from different cultures around the world, enhancing the **geography** curriculum.

Students can learn how **music** can enhance or subvert the meaning of moving images, create moods and announce genres.

The **art** curriculum makes increasing use of moving images and new media as key means of artistic expression.

A study of animation can also help students to engage with social and political ideas as part of the **citizenship** curriculum.

Many **science-**based concepts can be readily explained through animation and other moving image media.

Analysing stop-frame movement and pacing an animation require a solid grasp of numeracy and mental arithmetic, supporting **mathematics**.

In more general terms, the research project clearly indicated that the integration of animation into teaching and learning helps pupils to engage positively with schooling and increases motivation. Our findings also suggested that this promotes and engages a wider range of learning styles by:

- providing the opportunity for young people to pursue their interests, enthusiasm and different abilities or talents
- enhancing critical thinking, communication and problem-solving skills
- requiring teamwork and negotiation
- developing reasoning and risk-taking
- opening up new and innovative ideas
- increasing self-esteem
- learning visual concepts and communication
- learning new literacy to explore new terminologies
- equipping pupils for their future lives or career choices

It is time to make the curriculum relevant to students' lives outside schools and we hope this research helps bridge the widening gap between school and out-of-school learning experiences. Many students are immersed in the animation form via television, cinema, computer gaming and online content. They have an immediate connection to it and an intuitive sense, to some degree anyway, of how the form can function.

It is quite extraordinary that the majority of young people should go through their school careers with so little opportunity to study and engage with the most significant contemporary forms of culture and communication.

(David Buckingham, Media Education, Polity Press 2003)

Animation is a vibrant part of our everyday popular culture, appearing on television commercials, online content, computer gaming and in films. Animation can choose to mimic or step away from the world of realism. It's up to you and your filmmakers as to how much you stick with or depart from the real world. Animation is a playful medium. It takes the diversity, excitement and mystery of the world around us and brings it to vivid life.

As a starting point, think about the following kinds of animation approaches which are all very classroom friendly:

Plasticine animation: This can use the simplest to the most hi-tech approach. In class your best approach will probably be to use plasticine. Watch the *Wallace and Gromit* short films for inspiration. http://www.wallaceandgromit.com/

Cut-out animation: Make silhouette cut-out characters and place them against a lighter background. Watch *The Adventures of Prince Achmed* for inspiration. http://www.youtube.com/watch?gl=GB&v=25SP4ftxklg

Pixilation: The technique uses human performers who naturally, cannot stop moving. Get them to make still poses, like models and film them a frame at a time. Watch Norman McLaren's *Neighbours* for inspiration. http://www.nfb.ca/film/neighbours_voisins/

Drawn images: Use a pencil or marker pen or chalk to create a sequence of images on paper. Watch *Dangermouse* for inspiration. http://www.dangermouse.org/

USING THE TOOLKIT

The toolkit is designed as a mix and match resource, rather than a course to be followed in a linear fashion. The book is designed to be used alongside a **companion website**, which provides a series of closely related resources in the form of video clips and handouts.

Classroom activities are described via **worksheets.** These start with **teachers' notes**, which explain how to deliver the activity and often include a little background or historical information. Where appropriate, **extension work** linked to the activity is included here.

This is followed by a **materials** section listing the art materials, equipment and software needed to deliver the activity.

Finally, the **resources** section lists the **handouts** and **video clips** available on the **companion website.** These handouts can be printed and given out in class. They are a mixture of templates and activity guides with hints and tips to help the students undertake the classroom activities. Where the teacher might find them equally useful, we have included the handouts in the book as well.

The **Resources** section ends with lists of links to printed resources, websites and video clips which complement the subject.

Part One: Getting Started has two sub-sections. The first provides resources for exploring **Animation History**. The second offers **Beginners' Exercises** to help students gain an understanding of how animation works.

Part Two: Cineliteracy introduces ways to teach animation-based cineliteracy. It has four sub-headings: **The Language of Film and Animation, Exploring Genre, Music and Animation** and **Storytelling.**

Part Three: Animation Styles covers the various genres of animation that the research project tested in the classroom, with activities and practical tips to introduce each one.

Part Four: Schemes of Work presents three extended production projects around specific briefs, which were undertaken by 14- to 16-year-olds. The end results are included on the companion website to allow teachers an insight into the scope and quality of the finished work students can achieve in this time frame.

Part Five: Resources gives advice on where to find the equipment and software needed to run animation projects, and lists useful reference books and websites. For accurate up-to-date prices and information on the latest equipment, it is best to search online.

PART ONE: GETTING STARTED

1.1 ANIMATION HISTORY

WORKSHEET: SKETCHING A HISTORY OF ANIMATION

Teachers' note:
The following is intended as the basis for an introductory presentation on the history of animation.

We recommend viewing of some of the short clips listed in **A Brief History**, below. The resources section provides additional study links online.

It can also be engaging to follow this presentation with some of the practical exercises built around Victorian toys. The handouts are self-explanatory, but it helps to provide the suggested preambles, to place the toys in historical context. By making one or more of these, students can easily grasp the principle known as 'persistence of vision'.

Resources:
Video clip: **Animation History Presentation:** 🖱

Handout: **Animation History:** 🖱

Publication: **Understanding Animation** by Paul Wells, Routledge 1998 (available on Amazon http://www.amazon.co.uk/ Understanding-Animation-Paul-Wells/dp/0415115973/ref=sr_1_1?i e=UTF8&qid=1289465258&sr=8-1)

Internet links: **Persistence of Vision**
http://en.wikipedia.org/wiki/Persistence_of_vision

Edward Muybridge http://www.victorian-cinema.net/muybridge.htm

Optical Toys http://brightbytes.com/collection/phena.html

Museum of Childhood: Zoetrope
  http://www.vam.ac.uk/moc/collections/staff_picks/zoetrope/index.html

Online animated films and clips: see below in **A Brief History.**

Disclaimer:
As web links often expire we suggest the reader to simply Google
the film title again if the link no longer works.

A Brief History:
Over 35,000 years ago humans were making paintings on cave walls
and were sometimes drawing four pairs of legs to show motion.

Following this in 1600 BC, an Egyptian Pharaoh built a temple for his
goddess that had columns. Each column had a painted figure of the
goddess in a progressively changed position. To the horsemen and
charioteers riding past–the goddess appeared to move!

Simultaneously, the Ancient Greeks decorated pots with figures in successive stages of action–so by spinning the pot it created a sense of motion.

Over hundreds of years, people continued to make still images with the illusion of movement. Then, in 1824 a very important principle was discovered by a man named Peter Mark Roget–'the persistence of vision' theory. Persistence of Vision explains why our eyes are tricked into seeing movement. Our brain holds onto an image for a fraction of a second after the image has passed; if the eye sees a series of still images very quickly one after another, then the images will appear to move. Roget's theory gave birth to various optical contraptions.

After this there came a few other devices all based on the same theory. The one that you all will have seen is a flip book.

In fact, a flip book is the way that animators test their animation to see if the movement is correct, by flipping the pages before capturing them onto the computer.

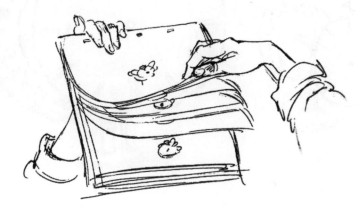

The animation toys shown on the handout help to trace the historical development of the medium. In the sixteenth century there were flip books in Europe and during the nineteenth century mechanisms were being developed and refined to create the illusion of movement.

The key moments in the development of animation technology include:

1824: the invention of the spinning card (Thaumatrope) by John Ayrton Paris or Peter Mark Roget.

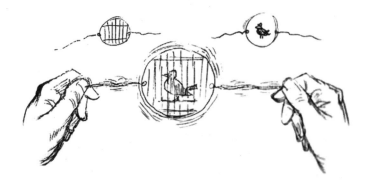

1831: the creation of the Spindle Viewer (Phenakistoscope) pioneered by Plateau.

1834: the creation of the Zoetrope by W. G. Horner.

1861: the creation of the Kinematoscope by Coleman Sellers.

1877: the creation of Reynard's Praxinoscope 1877.

Despite the rich variety of animation, worldwide audiences will equate animation with childhood visits to the cinema where their first movie was probably a Disney feature. As such, animation has tended to be narrowly regarded as kid's stuff when the evidence clearly indicates this is not true.

Throughout its history, animation has been used to explore wide-ranging adult themes, has been used as a medium for political allegory or propaganda, and in more recent times, has gained acceptance as a serious and important art form.

George Melies is often credited with making the first science fiction film, *Voyage to the Moon* in 1902. Its imaginative use of fantasy and special effects paved the way to the first experiments with animation, a few years later. Watch it here:
http://video.google.com/videoplay?docid=681138103275355387#

In 1906, J. Stuart Blackton produced *The Humorous Phases of Funny Faces* that is considered the first known attempt at stop-frame animation. Blackton incorporated drawn sequences that were shot frame by frame using a combination of blackboard, chalk and cut-outs for his animated forms. Watch it here:
http://www.youtube.com/watch?v=8dRe85cNXwg

The following year, Blackton produced another short film called *The Haunted Hotel*. The film used stop motion of three-dimensional objects. Wine was poured into a glass, bread was cut and a table was laid without apparent human agency. The film was very successful and helped popularize animation as a highly playful art form.

Emile Cohl who had been a successful comic strip artist made a short film called *Fantasmagorie* (1908) which film history tends to consider the first drawing-based animated film, a simple series of dreamlike images of stick figures. Watch it here:
http://vimeo.com/9231846

Cohl went on to produce hundreds of shorts but died in poverty. Others continued to explore the form such as Arthur Melbourne Cooper in his film *Dreams of Toyland* (1908) which animated real toys in a long-distance precursor to *Toy Story* (1995). View the complete 1908 film here (registration is needed):
http://www.screenonline.org.uk/film/id/1354093/

In the early years of the twentieth century in North America, cartoonist Winsor McCay moved into filmmaking and created the landmark short film *Gertie the Dinosaur.* Watch the film here:
http://video.google.com/videoplay?docid=746195425819461946#

No history of animation would be complete without a mention of the work of Walt Disney. Silly Symphonies is a series of 75 animated shorts, produced by his studio from 1929 to 1939. Watch The Three Little Pigs here: http://www.youtube.com/watch?v=Olo923T2HQ4

Alongside Disney the other high profile animation studio in America during the 1920s and 1930s was that of Dave and Max Fleischer. Indeed, it was the Fleischers who produced the first feature animation in documentary form, *The Einstein Theory of Relativity*. Watch it here: http://www.vintagetooncast.com/2006/11/einstein-theory-of-relativity.html

Based in New York, the Fleischer studio aesthetic was founded less on the realism that Disney pursued and much more on what writer Norman Klein, in his book *7 Minutes: The Life and Death of the American Cartoon*, calls turning the world upside down. The studio's greatest early success was the series Out of the Inkwell, which combined live action (an animator) and animation (a clown called Ko-Ko who climbed out of an inkwell and interacted with the animator). The studio would go on to produce *Popeye* and *Betty Boop*, which the Hays Code deemed too sexy and so, had to be toned down.

A Colour Box, 1935, by Len Lye is an advertisement for *'cheaper parcel post'*, and was screened to a general audience. It was made by painting vibrant abstract patterns on the film itself, and synchronizing them to a popular dance tune by Don Baretto and

His Cuban Orchestra. A panel of animation experts convened in 2005 by the Annecy film festival put this film among the top ten most significant works in the history of animation. Watch it here: http://www.dailymotion.com/video/x4r76e_a-color-box-len-lye-1935_creation

Russian animation has yielded classics such as *The Snow Queen*, adapted from the Hans Christian Andersen tale in 1959 by Lev Atamanov. It can be downloaded free here: http://www.archive.org/details/the_snow_queen_1959_animation

Norman McLaren's *Neighbours (1952)*, stands out as a landmark film from the same era, exploring pixilation techniques to unfold its Cold War allegory. Watch it here: http://nfb.ca/film/neighbours_voisins/

By the 1960s, though, the animated feature and short film in its full, classically animated sense began to give way to cheaper animation for television and for many what was considered the Golden Age had come to an end.

The late 1960s and through the 1970s were testing times, though of course shorter, more experimental work that was not dependent on armies of artists and animators continued. Consider, for example the abstract work of Oskar Fischinger and Robert Breer.

See an excerpt from Early Abstractions by Fischinger here: http://www.youtube.com/watch?v=RrZxw1Jb9vA

Watch '70' by Robert Breer here: http://www.youtube.com/watch?v=fcD3PS4Ckbwhttp://www.youtube.com/watch?v=fcD3PS4Ckbw

For the great Russian animator Yuri Norstein, animation is the place where allegory, entertainment and political comment enmesh. A timeless classic, typical of his style is Hedgehog in the Fog from 1975. Watch it with English sub-titles here: http://www.youtube.com/watch?v=smDlBmeeWck

The late 1970s and early 1980s saw brave and largely successful (if commercially failed) animated features occasionally being produced, notably *Watership Down* (Martin Rosen, 1977) based on the novel

by English author Richard Adams. Watch the trailer here:
http://www.youtube.com/watch?v=xZcHLpjiEdw

The 1980s also saw the emergence of computer animation, notably in the film *Tron* (Steven Lisberger, 1982) that is considered something of a cult piece. Watch the trailer here:
http://www.youtube.com/watch?v=3efV2wqEjE

In Canada, the National Film Board of Canada encouraged innovative approaches to animation and this has yielded a treasury of intriguing animation such as *The Street* (Caroline Leaf, 1976) an adaptation of a Mordecai Richler story in which a boy watches his sick grandma eventually die. Watch it here:
http://www.youtube.com/watch?v=54dm0Z99VOY

The extraordinary animation work of fellow Canadian, Ishu Patel, can be studied here: http://ishupatel.com/animation/index.html

Well worth a look is the beautiful work of Frederic Back. *The Man Who Planted Trees* (1987) tells the story of one shepherd's long and successful singlehanded effort to re-forest a desolate valley in the foothills of the Alps near Provence throughout the first half of the twentieth century. It can be viewed here:
http://www.viddler.com/explore/Ms_Valerie/videos/240/

Two of the most engrossing examples of animation in the 1990s were directed by Henry Selick: *The Nightmare Before Christmas* and *James and the Giant Peach*. His preferred medium of stop-motion animation was given a very high-profile platform and the audience for it was there, ready and waiting.

Watch the trailer for Nightmare Before Christmas here:
http://www.youtube.com/watch?v=kr5VuWeXGvQ

Watch the trailer for James and the Giant Peach here:
http://www.youtube.com/watch?v=BSbSC_k9rLg

Sometimes, animation in the short form especially has a liberty to explore and express thoughts and issues that larger film production-based material would struggle to. Take for example the Channel Four commission *A is for Autism* (1992 by Tim Webb) which is narrated by people with autism while images and sequences they have drawn illustrate the kinds of issues autism presents. A visual form makes a very complex psychology somehow understandable in its essentials. Watch it here: http://uk.video.yahoo.com/watch/2190791/6934786

In 1992 a collection of animated films was released through the British Film Institute called *Wayward Girls and Wicked Women*, a collection of animated shorts by female directors. It included films such as *The Stain* (Marjut Rimminen and Christine Roche, 1991) and *Daddy's Little Bit of Dresden China* (Karen Watson, 1988), films that both explored incest and abuse. For Jeanette Winterson, writing about this compilation, animation in its broadest application *'is closer to dance in its human delineation. It offers emotion freed from individual association, and yet is not abstract'.*

Order it here on VHS: http://www.amazon.co.uk/Wayward-Girls-Wicked-Women-Vol/dp/B00004CMOO/ref=sr_1_3?ie=UTF8&qid=1289491932&sr=1–3

Commercials and music videos have fuelled an appreciation of animation and often their handsome budgets have resourced very vivid pieces of work of which the music promo for the Peter Gabriel track *Sledgehammer* is often held up as an enduring example. Directed by Steve R. Johnstone, the video placed Gabriel in a range of fantastic scenarios that were created by different teams of animators. There was Aardman Animation (Peter Lord and David Sproxton), Richard Colesowski and the Brothers Quay, who were responsible for the sequence of Gabriel surrounded by fruit and vegetables for the *Fruit Cake* sequence. Aardman handled the stop motion of Gabriel hitting himself with hammers. The promo also included the pixilation technique, so that Gabriel had to strike a range of poses round which furniture was moved incrementally. Watch it here: http://www.youtube.com/watch?v=Y_E0bvOPTRg

This pixilation approach has also been used to eerie effect in Dave Borthwick's film *The Secret Adventures of Tom Thumb* (1993). Watch it here: http://www.youtube.com/watch?v=N3YKBOkfmbU

For further examples, organized according to style and genre, see **Recommended Animators** p. 150.

1.2 BEGINNERS' EXERCISES

HANDOUT: THE EASIEST ANIMATION

Draw two images that can make a sequence, with the second drawing directly beneath the first on the following page, for example, flapping wings, bird pecking.

In your sketchbook, left or right corner, cut carefully one slit with scissors.

The top piece can be rolled around a pencil to create movement by moving the pencil up and down quickly. Now drawing one and two create a moving sequence!!!

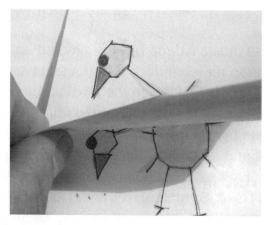

Two images of a pecking bird that make a sequence

Two images of a blinking frog that make a sequence

HANDOUT: CREATE A FLIP BOOK

Take a blank pad and on each corner create a stick figure that is performing a simple action such as walking. This flip book process is useful if you decide to create a fuller piece of hand-drawn animation later on. If you do not have a sketchbook, make your own book.

Materials:
A few sheets of paper, approx. 10cm x 10cm, and a stapler, or a small notebook as well as a pencil.

1. Staple the pages together at one edge to make a notebook. Sometimes a rubber band or string can work.
2. Draw a simple pin man on the last page of your notebook.
3. On the page before, trace the first pin man, but this time make his arms or legs move a small amount.
4. Continue tracing your previous drawing on the page before. Each time make his arms or legs move a small amount.

Drawing stick figures into the corner of a sketchbook

Be clear how many pictures you will have in your sequence. Twenty-five pictures is a good start as it demonstrates the amount of effort it takes to create 1 second of animation.

Flipping the sketchbook pages makes the animation move

It can help if you draw the first picture, the middle picture and the last picture initially as 'markers' and then go back and draw the inbetweens. When you have used up all the pages, flick the book from back to front to see the man move!

Draw pin men that run across pages, turn cartwheels or dance with partners!

Example:

Here's how to make a face go from a frown to a smile: On the last page of your pad draw your first picture. To make a face, draw a circle with two eyes. (You'll put in the mouth later.) Trace just the circle and the eyes onto all of the other pages. Those parts won't move. Now make the mouth. Start with drawing the happy mouth on the last page. Draw the mouth on each of the other pages, but each time you draw it make the line get flatter until it's a straight line. Then, make it bend in the other direction into a frown. You can colour in the background if you want to.

Flip the pages forwards and backwards to make your face smile and frown. Now you have your own mini-movie.

Now think of your own ideas. How about a scientific or geographic theme?

WORKSHEET: MAKE A SPINNING CARD (THAUMATROPE)

Teachers' note:

A thaumatrope is a toy that was popular in Victorian times. A disk or card with a picture on each side is attached to two pieces of string. When the strings are twirled quickly between the fingers the two pictures appear to combine into a single image due to persistence of vision. The invention of the thaumatrope, whose name means 'turning marvel' or 'wonder turner', has often been credited to the astronomer Sir John Herschel. However, it was a well-known London physicist, Dr. John A. Paris, who made this toy popular.

Thaumatropes were the first of many optical toys, simple devices that continued to provide animated entertainment until the development of modern cinema. Although the thaumatrope does not produce animated scenes, it relies on the same persistence of vision principle that other optical toys use to create illusions of motion. As the thaumatrope spins, the series of quick flashes is interpreted as one continuous image.

You might like to circulate the following handout, or simply explain the process to the class.

Materials:

Paper, pencil, scissors, strings and white cardboard

Resources:

http://en.wikipedia.org/wiki/Thaumatrope

HANDOUT: HOW TO MAKE A SPINNING CARD (THAUMATROPE)

Making a 'fish tank' spinning card

- Cut out a circle out of a white card
- Draw a picture of a fish on one side
- Flip the circle over and draw the fish tank on the other side.
- This drawing should be upside down
- Pierce one hole in each side of the circle
- Push a short length of string through each hole and double it up.
- Twist the strings, then spin the image.

A spinning card spinning

Drawings of a fish and a bowl

WORKSHEET: MAKE A SPINDLE VIEWER (PHENAKISTOSCOPE)

Teachers' note:

In 1832, Belgian physicist Joseph Plateau and his sons introduced the phenakistoscope ('spindle viewer'). Plateau's invention was a flat disk perforated with evenly spaced slots. Figures were drawn around the edges, depicting successive movements. A stick attached to the back allowed the disk to be held at eye level in front of a mirror. The viewer then spun the disk and watched the reflection of the figures pass through the slits, once again giving the illusion of movement.

Circulate the following handout and/or explain the process to the class.

Download and print one of the two templates in the resources section for each student to work with.

The resources section includes links to pages of image sequences and a book to help students with their drawing and analysis of movement.

Materials:

Card, scissors, ruler, mirror, black paint, glue, pencil, template (see below)

Resources:

Spindle Viewer template:

Phenakistoscope:
  http://en.wikipedia.org/wiki/Phenakistoscope
  http://courses.ncssm.edu/gallery/collections/toys/html/exhibit07.htm

Eadweard Muybridge:
  http://en.wikipedia.org/wiki/Eadweard_Muybridge

Thomas Edison, Kinetoscopic Record of a Sneeze:
  http://www.youtube.com/watch?v=2wnOpDWSbyw

Picturing Time: Work of Etienne-Jules Marey (1830–1904), Paperback
Available on Amazon here: http://www.amazon.co.uk/Picturing-Time-Etienne-Jules-Marey-1830–1904/dp/0226071758/ref=sr_1_1?ie=UTF8&qid=1289473328&sr=8–1

HANDOUT: HOW TO MAKE A SPINDLE VIEWER (PHENAKISTOSCOPE)

Cut out the template and stick it to a piece of card. Think about drawing one shape that moves around, turns, stretches or grows. Working with colour can be very effective. You can also work with three different shapes. One at the outside of the wheel, one in the middle section and one on the inside. How about a bird flying, a walk cycle, a horse, cat or other animal walk?

When you have drawn your sequence of images, cut out the slits with scissors or a sharp knife. Paint the opposite side black. Make a spindle with a sharp pencil, pushed into the axis, black side facing you. Spin the phenakistoscope in front of a mirror, looking through the slits.

If you prefer not to draw, try a photo-based face animation. Use a digital camera, tripod and the photo printing wizard. (Most economical is to choose contact sheet prints or wallet prints.) Set up a camera on a tripod. Once set up it should stay still.

You can use your own face, and make a sequence from sad to happy to sad. Keep in mind it must take 10 or 12 pictures to cycle back to where you started.

WORKSHEET: MAKING AN ANIMATION
WHEEL (ZOETROPE)

Teachers' note:

Originally called the 'Wheel of the Devil', the zoetrope or animation wheel is a moving image machine that was invented in the 1830s. In the 1860s, it was manufactured and marketed to the public. It was then that it was given the name zoetrope, from the Greek zoa (living things) and trope (turning). Zoetropes were extremely popular forms of entertainment for both children and adults in the Victorian era. Long slits of paper with sequential drawings are placed inside the cylinder and spun while looking through the slit. These started selling in 1867 in the USA as toys. The cylinder is cut with a vertical slit at equal intervals. Beneath the slits, inside the cylinder, is a strip with frames of slightly differently positioned images–for example a person waling. Spin the cylinder, look through the slits and see the illusion of movement. The earliest zoetrope was made in China around 180 AD by Ting Huan and was driven by convection and hung over a lamp. The rising air turned vanes at the top of the device and see-through paper was hung with pictures on them. The images appeared to move.

The class can make a zoetrope wheel from scratch using one of the worksheets listed in the links below. Alternatively, you can buy classroom-friendly zoetrope kits from the listed supplier.

When the class is drawing their strips to place inside the wheel, help them choose simple transformations or moving figures that are within their abilities. You can offer the same advice contained in the handout for the spindle viewer.

Materials:

White card, glue, scissors, zoetrope strip template

Resources:

Zoetrope Strip Template:

Construction guides:
   http://www.sonypictures.com/classics/shadowmagic/zoetrope/pdf/
      instructions.pdf

http://www.the-making-place.co.uk/pages/zoe.html

Zoetrope kits for the classroom:
  http://www.leons-craft-workshops.co.uk/other-zoetrope-kit.php

Viewing images in a spinning zoetrope

WORKSHEET: BREATHE LIFE INTO TEDDY

Teachers' note:
This can either be used as a simple drawing exercise, or as a template for a cut-out puppet. If you use it to create puppets, this can lead naturally onto the cut-out animation exercises to be found in Part Three.

Copy the template and ask your students to draw and colour in teddy's features. The template can be glued to a piece of card before students cut out the different parts and fix them together with BluTak or paper fasteners. They might also want to experiment with different poses and different shapes for the body parts.

Materials:
Glue, thin card, scissors, template

Resources:
Handout: Teddy template:

WORKSHEET: TWIST'EM, BEND'EM, SQUASH'EM

Teachers' note:

This is a simple drawing exercise that can be used as a warm-up before trying some simple-drawn animation work. The basic shapes in the handout can be used as the basic building blocks for characters and forms.

Alternatively, just ask the class to begin by drawing a circle, an oblong, a square and a triangle on a large sheet of paper, with plenty of space between each one.

Suggest the following: Can you extend some of the shapes into the third dimension? Can you redraw a shape with a bend or twist in it, or as it would look if squashed? Think of the shapes as if they were made of modelling clay!

Draw some different basic shapes, then try transforming those into characters.

Encourage the students to work with simple confident strokes and to resist using an eraser. It is not about right or wrong, it's about building up confidence in drawing.

Materials:

Pencils, white A4 or A3 photocopy paper or sketchpads

Resources:

Handout: Basic Shapes:

WORKSHEET: EXPRESSIVE LINES AND CHARACTERS

Teachers' note:

These basic exercises are designed to break the ice with students who say 'but I can't draw!' Their purpose is to introduce the approach of the cartoonist, who can use the simplest of lines to express human emotions and begin to tell stories. It also helps students realize that, by applying their imaginations, they can start to bring characters to life with the simplest of drawing techniques.

Copy the handouts or ask the students to start by filling a blank page with ovals and squares. Now ask them to add few lines to each shape to either express an emotion or transform the shape into a recognizable object or character. The second handout suggests specific emotions. The character sheets can be used as templates to help with basic character design.

Once the class is feeling a little more confident, invite them to start designing characters from scratch in their sketchbooks. Choose one emotion, such as angry, and ask the class to spend 10 minutes drawing a range of angry facial expressions and gestures for their characters. Suggest they get the **body** to show the emotion. Repeat the exercise with different emotions.

The point of this is to:

- learn how to draw quickly and loosely
- express emotions with the whole figure, not just the face

Materials:
Pencils, A4 or A5 photocopy paper or sketchbooks

Resources:
Expressive Lines handout:

Creating Expressions:

Character Sheet 1:

Character Sheet 2:

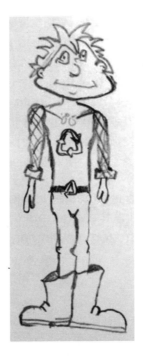

WORKSHEET: GETTING THE BASICS OF MOVEMENT

Teachers' note:

These drawing exercises have two main objectives. First, they help students to start analysing movement and transformation through their drawing. Secondly, they help them develop a confident and relaxed approach to drawing, essential for drawn animation. In developing a personal style, students will find a big sketchbook very helpful. They can use it to keep a record of their developing ideas, and to get used to thinking and expressing themselves visually. Invite them to take every opportunity to observe and sketch character and movement. In this way they will begin to develop a vocabulary of gestures and expressions. Suggest they sketch people walking, waving or dancing. If they find drawing anatomy daunting, suggest an abstract theme or simpler forms, which focus on the expressive power of line, form, shape and colour.

You could begin by using the Drawing Simple Transformations handout. Next ask the students to work directly in their sketchbooks. An excellent point of departure is to set up a quick character sketch activity, working to a strict time frame. Get a stopwatch or a clock and set it up next to you. Ask the students to sharpen their pencils, and hide their erasers. Give them 1 minute to draw one full figure character from imagination. Remind them that softer pencils allow a faster drawing style, but have to be sharpened more often, which can break concentration. A 2B pencil is a good compromise.

Repeat the exercise for 15 minutes or longer, then review the results. With each new drawing, ask the students to make their character adopt a different pose or frozen movement, such as jumping, flying, playing golf etc.

Extension work:

For further research invite the students to search the internet for inspiration from the following great artists and animators:

Leonardo da Vinci: his drawings of moving figures

Raphael: his drawings of moving figures

Edgar Degas: his paintings of ballet dancers

Joanna Quinn: her animated men and women in the short films *Girls Night Out* and *Body Beautiful*

Mario Minichiello: narrative drawings

Gerald Scarfe: narrative drawings

Preston Blair's guidebooks to character design and animation

Materials:
Pencils, A4 or A5 photocopy paper or sketchpads

Resources:
Handout: Drawing Simple Transformations:
Short videos about drawing:
   http://www.andysanimation.co.uk/Pages/DrawingVideos.html

An online drawing course:
   http://www.karmatoons.com/drawing/drawing.htm

A page of links to drawing resources:
   http://www.artshow.com/resources/drawing.html

A video showing how to draw mad scientist and Frankenstein character designs:
   http://www.youtube.com/watch?v=1R5izhTr7ko&feature=related

PART TWO: CINELITERACY

2.1 THE LANGUAGE OF FILM AND ANIMATION

Cineliteracy is the understanding and appreciation of film or 'moving image texts'. It is the development of skills in reading, comprehending and judging moving images and sound both intellectually and emotionally. Understanding animation as one type of moving image text is referred to as animation literacy. This toolkit aims to reflect the role animation has in students' lives and to offer some suggestions on how this interest can be used to build on an understanding of animation literacy.

Through animation we can explore a wide range of social, cultural and personal issues. Animation projects can be readily integrated into any curriculum subject. Why not develop a maths and animation project for example? Animation can involve and illustrate complex ideas, relevant to any study area.

Like any cultural product, animation can be considered historically, economically, aesthetically, technologically and in terms of a given production context. All of these approaches have a place in cineliteracy.

An understanding of cineliteracy is a key part of the media component of the English National Curriculum. The Focus of Learning charts on pp. 34–35 are based on the English National Curriculum guidelines for Key Stage 3 and 4 (ages 11–16).

The three themes of cineliteracy are:

- Film Language
- Producers and Audiences
- Messages and Values

The toolkit examines these themes in a number of ways, to demonstrate how an understanding of cineliteracy can be woven into classroom projects. A typical example is Scheme of Work 3: Music Videos (p. 117) in which the students use the language and grammar of film in creative ways, while targeting particular audiences. See also Scheme of Work 2: TV Ads (p. 112) where the student work conveys clear messages and values to the intended audiences.

In the rest of this section you will find a series of worksheets designed to explore cineliteracy through the study of animation. For a more detailed approach to teaching cineliteracy in the classroom, embracing film, television and animation, try the resources below.

Resources:
Focus of Learning Charts (pp. 34–35)

Publication: Story Shorts: A Resource for Key Stage 2 Literacy (BFI Education). Buy it on DVD or VHS here: http://www.bfi.org.uk/education/teaching/storyshorts/

Publication: Look Again! A teaching guide to using film and television with 3- to 11-year-olds (BFI Education). Free download here: http://www.bfi.org.uk/education/teaching/lookagain/

Publication: Moving Images in the Classroom (BFI Education). http://www.bfi.org.uk/education/teaching/miic/

CINELITERACY CONCEPT	FOCUS OF LEARNING	FOCUS OF LEARNING	FOCUS OF LEARNING
	KS 3 Year 7 Age 11	**KS 3 Year 8 Age 12**	**KS 3 Year 9 Age 13**
FILM LANGUAGE	For year 7 pupils the key concerns of Film Language centre on issues of how a narrative story is structured and how images and sounds work together. Hence, your classwork would be concerned with discussing a film in terms of music, location, interior and exterior settings and the role of actors and performance.	Film Language focuses on the differences between film, video and television and allows scope for comparative study. Furthermore, how meaning is constructed through the editing of image and sound. Identifying major media styles and narrative forms is also central as is the ways in which style relates to technology.	Film Language looks at how film, TV and video styles and narrative forms can relate to authors, the production context and the social and cultural context.
PRODUCERS AND AUDIENCES	Explore the importance of genre to our understanding of films. There is also a consideration of the intended audience of a film text and how differing audiences bring differing responses to a given film text.	The key concern here is with the relationship between understanding the demands of pre production, production, post production and exhibition and how these issues relate to matters of creation, influence, intent and response to a film.	Producers and Audiences there is the aim to describe and explain how authors, genres and stars generate meaning. Pupils are also encouraged to identify and describe some of the ways in which film, video and television institutions relate to social, cultural and political contexts. Pupils will also need to relate distribution, exhibition and audience.
MESSAGES AND VALUES	Messages and Values concerns the class with being able to identify the level of realism to which a film aims and where the line between the real and the fantastic can be drawn. This is a particular area of interest in terms of animation.	Messages and Values of a film are considered in terms of how social groups, events and ideas are represented. Pupils are also encouraged to explain and justify judgements and personal responses and argue for alternative ways of representing a group event or idea. Pupils are also encouraged to discuss and evaluate texts with strong social or ideological messages.	The focus is on discussing the ideological messages in mainstream texts. Pupils must also describe and analyse different levels of realism on offer (visual and emotional realism—the choices a character makes and their reaction to events). Finally, pupils should engage with explaining the relationship between aesthetic style and social and political meaning.

	FILM LANGUAGE	PRODUCERS AND AUDIENCES	MESSAGES AND VALUES
KS 4 Year 10–11 Age 14–15	Experiences and Activities: Film Language pupils should see a range of film, video, television (FVT) that both consolidates and extends existing viewing experience in terms of genre, directors, national cinemas, mainstream and non-mainstream and historical periods. Pupils should also find out more about different modes of FVT production eg industrial / mainstream vs low budget independent. Pupils should have opportunities to relate FVT knowledge to other cultural fields such as literature, history, fine art and music. Pupils should be able to investigate a topic using FVT text, online and print sources. Outcomes: Identify and describe some major FVT styles and narrative forms, using key words. Explain how elements of FTV styles may relate to technologies, eg portable cameras, editing software.	Identify and discuss some of the factors in the production process that may effect the final shape and meaning of a FTV text. Describe some of the risks and costs involved in FVT production, distribution and exhibition. Explain some of the possibilities and limitations of audience research.	Meanings and Values/Messages and Values: Use key words to discuss and evaluate FVT texts with strong social or ideological messages. Use ICT to redraft and manipulate moving image and sound sequences in response to audience comment. Use FVT knowledge to evaluate information on FVT from online and print sources. Use stills and clips in live or recorded presentations of critical arguments or investigations.

WORKSHEET: THE GRAMMAR OF FILM LANGUAGE

Teachers' note:

Begin the session by explaining the basic syntax that makes up the grammar of film language. Just as literature comprises of a text-based grammar, film has a grammar built upon image, sound and montage in order to create expression, thought and meaning.

Any film is comprised of **shots** that build into **scenes**. **Scenes** are combined to create **sequences** and these, in turn link to make a complete **film**.

There are three fundamental **shot types** that you will always want to use in various combinations. Any combination of these three key shots will allow you to tell a story in moving images. A director normally chooses the shot type which best conveys a particular point, detail, mood or gesture to carry the story forwards. These examples were drawn by a group of 7-year-olds, and are stills from the short film Bubbletown (see p. 97).

- A WIDE SHOT will typically introduce and establish a location and time.

- A MID-SHOT will allow you a more detailed or specific look at the action.

- A CLOSE-UP will offer a detail that might carry a particular emotional or intellectual resonance.

Copy and circulate the Film Grammar Handout.

Screen a 1-minute clip from an animated film. Ask the students to use the handout to count the number of wide, medium and close-up shots they see in the clip. There is unlikely to be a consensus, as many shots sit on the borderline between close-up and medium shot, or medium and wide. This doesn't matter, as the point of the exercise is to take a first step towards deconstructing the media text.

Now ask the pupils to select particular shots of each type, and discuss their impact on the viewer.

- Why did the director choose this type of shot at this moment?
- What does this shot tell us?
- What kinds of visual information can be seen in the composition?
- How does it help to convey the story?
- What kind of emotional impact does the shot have?

Finally, ask the group to imagine the next three shots in the story you were just watching. They must decide if these will be wide shots, medium shots or close-ups, then sketch them in the three boxes at the bottom of the handout.

Ask individuals to justify their choices. This will help the students to begin using film language creatively and appropriately, and will provide a good foundation to any storyboarding they might do later.

Materials:
Pens or pencils

Resources:
Handout: Film Grammar: 🖱

Any clip from an animated film

WORKSHEET: DECONSTRUCTING A MEDIA TEXT

Teachers' note:

This exercise will help students to develop a deeper understanding of the language of the moving image. Groundwork like this will reap many benefits when they begin to tackle practical projects.

A first step towards this understanding is to provide students with a framework for deconstructing an animated short and reading it as a moving image text.

Choose a short animation that you feel will engage the class.

Ask the students to discuss the film by considering each of these topics in turn. Don't be afraid to rerun the film or a sequence several times, looking at a different aspect of its construct each time.

Camera:

Consider the style of camerawork used in the opening sequence. Find examples of different shot types such as extreme close-ups, close-ups, medium or wide shots. Why were these types of shots used and to what purpose?

Colour:

Describe the colour palette. How does the use of colour relate to the story and mood of the film? Do different colours and combinations of colour provoke different emotions and if so, why? If it's a black and white film, why did the director choose this approach?

Character:

How is each character introduced in the film? What does his or her appearance tell you about their personalities? What do their gestures and movements tell us about their personalities and motives in the story? Are they like real-life people? If not, how are they different?

Story:

How does the story begin? How does the story end and resolve itself? How does the storyline motivate the actions of the characters? Do you like the characters and can you identify with their story?

Sound:

What sounds can you hear in the animation? Can you hear sound effects? What is their purpose? Do you hear people talking? Why? Are there different ways the characters communicate with each other? Is there any silence? Is there music? What instruments can you hear? Does the music help tell the story?

Settings:

Where does the story take place? How do you know? Is it a particular country? Does it remind you of anywhere you have been? What are the main settings in the film? List them. How do they help to tell the story? What do the settings and props tell us about the characters?

Materials:

Data Projector, whiteboard or screen and sound

Resources:

Any short animation clip of 1–3 minutes (see **A Brief History** for links, p. 9 or **Recommended Animators** p. 150)

WORKSHEET: FREEZE FRAME

Teachers' note:

This exercise is another approach to deconstructing a media text. By looking at single frames from a film, rather than sequences, students sometimes find it easier to consider particular aspects of a film's construct. These include the composition of the scene, the position of actors, use of props, use of lighting and positioning of cameras.

The key point of the exercise is to encourage students to analyse the reasoning behind the director's or lighting cameraperson's decisions, and to consider the potential impact of changing any aspects of these.

Choose a short animation clip on DVD that can be stopped at random intervals. Choose a variety of frames that employ different camera angles and shot types.

Questions:

- What can you see in the 'frozen image'?
- How are the elements of the image organized within the frame?
- Why is the shot composed like this?
- What difference would it make if it were composed differently?
- How does lighting and colour affect what you see?
- How does the lighting contribute to the atmosphere of the shot?
- Where do you think the camera is, and why is it placed where it is?
- What other clues are contained within the frame that help to tell the story?
- What do they tell us about the time/place/setting?
- What can you tell about the characters from how they are dressed?
- What information can be gained about the characters from their dress and body language?

This type of analysis is closely linked to the French theory of mise-en-scene. When applied to the cinema, it refers to everything that appears before the camera and how it is organized.

Mise en scene therefore encompasses both what the audience can see, and the way in which we are invited to see it. It refers to many major elements of communication in the cinema, and the combination through which they operate expressively.

(John Gibbs, Mise en scene: Film Style and
Interpretation, 2002)

Materials:
Data Projector, whiteboard or screen and sound

Resources:
Any short animation clip of 1–3 minutes (see **A Brief History** for
   links, p. 9)

Publication: Mise-en-Scene: Film Style and Interpretation (Short
   Cuts) by John Gibbs, Wallflower Press 2001. Available on Amazon
   here: http://www.amazon.co.uk/Mise-en-Scene-Film-Style-
   Interpretation-Short/dp/190336406X/ref=sr_1_1?ie=UTF8&s=book
   s&qid=1289815686&sr=8–1

WORKSHEET: STUDYING A TITLE SEQUENCE

Teachers' note:

A title sequence is more than just a list of credits. It can be a mini-movie which sets up the film that it's a part of. It can establish mood, period and style. A title sequence can take care of backstory. It can soothe the audience or get them agitated. Title sequences are an art form of their own

(Deborah Allison, 'Promises in the Dark: Opening Title Sequences in American Feature Films of the Sound Period.' Big Film Design)

In this activity students are encouraged to develop their analytical skills by deconstructing the title sequence from one of the feature films listed below. Tell the students nothing about the film before they view the sequence. Ask them to consider these questions and explain their reasoning.

- What do you think this is a title sequence for? (feature film, TV, short film, etc.)
- Can you tell what it is going to be about from the title sequence?
- Who is the target audience? (children, teens, adults, specialist audience, etc.)
- Does it follow a narrative or is it more visually driven?
- What do you think is the purpose of a title sequence?
- Does this title sequence work well?

An interesting variation on this exercise is to cover the video screen and ask students to listen carefully to the soundtrack. Ask them to describe what they hear. Next, ask them to analyse each of the different sonic elements in turn, by posing these questions:

About music:

How would you describe this music?

What feelings and images does it suggest to you? How does the music contribute to the meaning of a sequence? How would the sequence be affected if the music were absent or different?

About sound effects:
What exactly can you hear?

Are the sound effects used simply to represent an action or do they contribute to the drama of the sequence?

About words:
What can you tell about the actors from their tone of voice and what they say? How does intonation, accent, volume contribute to your impressions of the actor?

About silence:
Why do you think the sequence is silent at this point?

How can silence create drama/atmosphere/tension?

About the sequence as a whole:
What difference does the sound make to the sequence?

What difference would it make if either the music or sound effects were missing? How does sound and image combine to create specific meanings? What contribution is made by each individual element? Do these elements change over time? If so, what do the changes mean?

Finally, show the sound and image together and discuss how seeing the image changes one's understanding of the use of sound.

Materials:
Data Projector, whiteboard or screen and sound

Resources:
Corpse Bride, Tim Burton

Spirited Away, The Studio Ghibli Collection

Belleville Rendez-Vous, Sylvain Chomet

Peter and the Wolf, Breakthrough Films, Director Suzie Templeton

The Sun Was Lost, Monoru Maeda

Lemony Snicket's A Series of Unfortunate Events, Brad Silberling

(All these titles are available on DVD from Amazon. See also
   Recommended Animators p. 150.)

WORKSHEET: WHO MAKES ANIMATIONS?

Teachers' note:
This exercise is designed to provide students with an insight into the
many different job roles within the animation and film industry.

View the end credits of a popular animation. Ask the students to
research a particular job or role in the making of the film that they
saw in the credits (e.g. director, producer, animator, script writer
sound designer).

Ask each student to make an information leaflet about the job role,
in the form of a job description. Invite students to describe this role
to the rest of the class.

Materials:
Data Projector, whiteboard or screen and sound, exercise books,
pens

Resources:
See previous exercise

WORKSHEET: PITCHING AN IDEA

Teachers' note:

This exercise provides an excellent structure to help students devise an idea and outline treatment for their animation project. It need not be used solely in this context, as the format will help in the planning of any film or animation. It also encourages students to work and think as a team to pitch their treatment to a panel of commissioning editors.

Divide the class into groups of five to six students. Set each group the task of designing a treatment for a pilot for a new series of animated shorts for a children's channel. Their plans should then be presented to another group acting as commissioning editors for the children's television channel.

When presenting their treatment or 'pitch', the production teams should try to structure their presentation and ideas for maximum, persuasive effect.

Questions the commissioning editors might ask:

- Why did you choose this target audience?
- What do you think they will like about the animation?
- How will the content and subject matter engage the audience?
- What do you think makes your idea suitable for and attractive to the target audience?
- How will you get people to watch your film?
- How will it be marketed?
- How does the idea relate to other children's animations already being screened? What makes it different?
- What factors did you consider as you planned your product?

Materials:
Sketchbooks, pens, pencils

Resources:
Handout: Writing a Treatment

HANDOUT: WRITING A TREATMENT

Once you've come up with your basic film idea, prepare a treatment. A treatment would normally be given to potential financiers or producers to get the film made. It's a description of the story, including atmosphere, style and setting. It tells the audience how they will experience the film in images and sounds.

Here is a framework for your treatment:

Title: This is the working title for your film or film series.

Strap line: This is one sentence that explains the purpose of your film.

Approximate length: The final edited length in minutes

Synopsis: The synopsis should try to answer the following questions:

What happens in your story? Describe the main characters, the task or quest they are undertaking and how it is resolved.

Who is your audience? Who are you making this film for? (This question is very important as it will inform the style and content of your film.)

How will the film be structured? Describe the shape and sequence of the film. How will the different scenes and sequences be organized and relate to each other?

What will the audience see and hear? Describe the location and 'world' of your film. List the different settings in which the action takes place. Describe the different types of imagery you plan to include in the film. What visual style will you adopt?

Will you use a narrator, and if so what will be the narrator's role? Will the characters use dialogue to help develop the story?

Will you use music and if so, what style?

2.2 EXPLORING GENRE

WORKSHEET: EXPLORING GENRE

Teachers' note:

Genres are different types of film and animation, defined by the kind of stories they tell and the production style. For example, we know that a science fiction film tells a different kind of story to a romantic comedy. Interestingly, you can combine genres.

Below is a list of commonplace genres and suggested definitions. (You might like to print, hand out and discuss these definitions in class, and consider other variations or hybrids.)

Show an animated film with a clearly identifiable genre, stopping before the climax. Based on their knowledge of the story so far, invite students to make predictions about how the film will end. After the real ending is revealed students should reflect on their reasons for their predictions.

Ask the following:

- What genre/s does the film belong to?
- How close were your predictions to the actual ending?
- Was the ending typical of this genre?
- Were the main characters typical of this genre?

Invite the class to write a synopsis for the story, but this time adapted to another genre of their choosing. Invite students to read out the results and discuss with the class.

Extension work: adapt the synopsis into a six-shot storyboard.

Storyboarding in progress

Materials:

Data Projector, whiteboard or screen and sound, paper and pens

Resources:

Any genre-specific animation. (See **A Brief History** p. 9 for examples.)

Handout: Genres

HANDOUT: GENRES

What does the word **genre** mean?

Genres are different types of film and animation, defined by the kind of stories they tell and the production style. For example, we know that a science fiction film tells a different kind of story to a romantic comedy. Interestingly, you can combine genres. Below is a list of commonplace genres and suggested definitions. (You might like to discuss these definitions and consider other variations.)

- Crime: places its character within realm of criminal activity.
- Film noir: portrays its principal characters in a nihilistic and existentialist realm or manner.
- Historical: taking place in the past amidst notable historical circumstances.
- Science fiction: a setting or plot defined by the effects of speculative (not yet existing) technology for example future space travel, cyberpunk, time travel.
- Sports: sporting events and locations pertaining to a given sport.
- War: battlefields and locations pertaining to a time of war.
- Western: films set in wilderness on the verge of civilization, usually in the American West.
- Action: generally involves a moral interplay between 'good' and 'bad' played out through violence or physical force.
- Adventure: involving danger, risk and/or chance, often with a high degree of fantasy.
- Comedy: intended to provoke laughter.
- Drama: mainly focused on character development and interplay.
- Fantasy: speculative fiction outside reality (e.g. involving myths and legends).
- Horror: intended to provoke fear in audience.
- Slasher: A variation of Horror that focuses less on suspense and more on death and gore; also called Splatter film.

- Mystery: the progression from the unknown to the known by discovering and solving a series of clues.

- Romance: dwelling on the elements of romantic love.

- Thrillers: intended to provoke excitement and/or nervous tension in the audience.

- Documentary: based on events that happened in real life.

- Musical: songs are sung by the characters and interwoven into the narrative.

WORKSHEET: GENRE TRANSLATION

Teachers' note:

In this exercise, students translate a moving image text for example a documentary, animation, news item, TV commercial or scene from a feature film—into a print genre such as a newspaper item, a magazine feature, an extract from a novel, a short story or a poem.

Another option is to give the students a printed text and ask them to convert it into moving image form, first as script or storyboard, and then if possible as video (as a brief extract or 'try-out' of one scene).

The purpose of the exercise is to develop insights into how the medium affects the message and the way it is conveyed to its intended audience. It can prompt discussion of how meaning can change when information is presented in different forms or transposed to another medium. Each medium has its own language, conventions and genres. The moving image is more appropriate for some kinds of content or structure and the written, printed word is more appropriate for others.

The exercise should prompt questions such as:

- What can you say in print that you cannot tell or show in moving images?
- What can you show in moving images that you cannot convey in print?
- What kinds of story, information and ideas are best told in print and what are
- best told in moving images?

Materials:

Sketchbooks or exercise books, pens, pencils

Resources:

An article from a recent newspaper or magazine, or

A video clip from broadcast television, or

An animation clip (See **A Brief History** p. 9 for suggestions)

Students watching an animation

WORKSHEET: GENRE AND CHARACTER DESIGN

Teachers' note:

This exercise looks at the relationships between genre and character in the context of one of the best-known animation series on television: *The Simpsons.*

Screen an episode of *The Simpsons*. Look at the genre handout and consider how many of these genres the series as a whole falls within. Consider how the main characters support these genre definitions through their personalities and actions.

Next look at each of the main characters in turn.

- Homer–father, lazy, overweight but likeable nuclear plant worker
- Marge–mother, housewife and community do-gooder
- Bart–10-year-old anarchist and vandal with a good heart
- Lisa–8-year-old super achiever, feminist, vegetarian and social activist
- Baby Maggie–quietly sucking her pacifier

Discuss the visible attributes of each character and what each tells us about them. Why do you think Marge has blue hair? What objects do Bart and Lisa own and what do they say about them?

Invite each student to select one of these characters and devise a character sheet for him or her. (They can use the Handout: Character Sheet 3, or start from scratch in a sketchbook.)

You might like to download and print the Handouts: Character Design Sheets 4 and 5 to provide an example from the finished film, A Decent Excuse, also available as a downloadable clip.

Offer the following tips and advice:

When designing characters you need to fully understand their personalities and imagine how they will behave in a range of situations. The more things you know about the character the more convincing it will be for the audience and the greater the bond they'll have with the character and the story.

Discuss the character sheets with the class.

Materials:
Sketchbooks or exercise books, pens, pencils

Resources:
Handouts: Character Sheet 3, 4 and 5

Video Clip: A Decent Excuse by Julian Frank

2.3 MUSIC AND ANIMATION

WORKSHEET: MUSIC AND IMAGERY IN *PETER AND THE WOLF*

Teachers' note:

This and the following two worksheets offer good ways to prompt discussion about the power of music to help tell a story in animation, to enhance mood and atmosphere and to help develop characterization.

In 2006, Suzie Templeton directed a modernized, stop-motion animated adaptation of *Peter and the Wolf.* It is unusual in its lack of any dialogue or narration, the story being told purely in images and sound and interrupted by sustained periods of silence. The soundtrack is performed by The Philharmonia Orchestra, and the film received its premiere with a live accompaniment in the Royal Albert Hall. The film won the Annecy Cristal and the Audience Award at the 2007 Annecy International Animated Film Festival.

Begin by asking the students to listen carefully to part of the soundtrack of *Peter and the Wolf,* without the visuals. Ask the following:

What type of film you think this is? What style do you think it is? What genre? Does the music invite you to see the film? Does it give away the theme or style? Does the music set a target audience?

How would you describe this music? What feeling/images does it suggest to you? How does the music contribute to the mood/meaning of a sequence? How would the sequence be affected if the music were absent/different?

Next, show the complete film, including both image and sound. Ask the following:

About the sound effects: What exactly can you hear? Are the sound effects used simply to represent an action or do they contribute to the drama of the sequence?

About the music: What can you tell about the characters from the music which accompanies them? How does the melody, tempo and style of the music contribute to your impressions of the character?

About silence: Why do you think the sequence is silent at this point? How can silence create drama, atmosphere or tension?

About sound and image together: What difference does the sound make to the sequence? What difference would it make if either the music or sound effects were missing? How do sound and image combine to create specific effects? What contribution is made by the individual elements? Does the sound/music change? What do the changes mean? (e.g. changes in volume or tempo).

Extension work: ask the students to write a synopsis for the film.

Materials:
Sketchbooks or exercise books, pens, pencils

Resources:
DVD video: *Peter and the Wolf* directed by Suzie Templeton

Available on Amazon here: http://www.amazon.co.uk/Sergei-Prokofievs-Peter-Wolf-DVD/dp/B001RNXZ06/ref=sr_1_2?ie=UTF8&qid=1289826303&sr=8–2

http://en.wikipedia.org/wiki/Peter_and_the_Wolf

http://www.philtulga.com/Peter.html

WORKSHEET: UNDERSTANDING LEITMOTIV IN
PETER AND THE WOLF

Teachers' note:
There are three strands of aural support for any film – dialogue, music and sound effects – with the latter dividing into foley (specific sounds, such as footsteps) and atmosphere (setting the aural landscape, for example, wind in the trees). Sound effects deal with realistic aural landscapes whereas music makes a powerful contribution to a film by implication and association. It supports and develops the narrative, adding to the emotional temperature and sometimes creating links with specific characters or circumstances (leitmotiv).

Generally, music is added to film at a later stage in production. However in the case of the production of *Peter and the Wolf*, the music and the narrative came first. Consequently the director Suzie Templeton had to reverse the process of film production by creating visuals to fit the music.

The music was recorded earlier in pre-production with the Philharmonia Orchestra conducted by Mark Stephenson. The 24-track recording aimed for a highly characterful, spirited interpretation. After recording, the music was analysed note-by-note and transcribed onto a frame-by-frame bar chart. The film is made at 25 frames per second; therefore the film is made up of a total of about 45,000 frames. The bar chart enabled the director and animator to synchronize animation with the music.

Peter and the Wolf is scored for flute, oboe, clarinet in A, bassoon, three horns, trumpet, trombone, timpani, triangle, tambourine, cymbals, castanets, snare drum, bass drum and strings. Prokofiev uses the rising 2nd inversion major triad in the themes for Peter, the bird and the cat. Also, all character parts apart from the grandfather start on the fifth of the scale.

Prokofiev's own thoughts were that: *'The role of each animal or bird will be played by a single instrument, but the many-sided human character will be, say, a string quartet . . . Yes, we should begin with specific striking contrasts: the wolf and the bird, the evil and the good, the big and the small. The characters will be expressed in the timbres of different instruments and each of them will have a leitmotiv.'*

Show the film to the class. Ask the students to identify the use of leitmotiv. Which instruments are used for each character?

- Peter
- Grandfather
- Duck
- Crow
- Wolf
- Hunter

Does each musical passage suit the character it accompanies? What links can you find between each character and its music?

The exercise should help students to understand the process of composing musical material for a film. The commercial process of adding music to film is highly sophisticated, however the principles are relatively simple.

Materials:
Data Projector, whiteboard or screen and sound, paper and pens

Resources:
Peter and the Wolf directed by Suzie Templeton

Available on Amazon here: http://www.amazon.co.uk/Sergei-Prokofievs-Peter-Wolf-DVD/dp/B001RNXZ06/ref=sr_1_2?ie=UTF8&qid=1289826303&sr=8–2

WORKSHEET: COMPOSE A 15-SECOND LEITMOTIV

Teachers' note:

This activity is a creative music-making exercise, allowing students to begin composing music for a particular character, place or idea. Ask the students to each select one of these animal haikus as a starting point for the composition.

The Wolf

A silver grey wolf

Howls an eerie, spooky howl

Staring at the moon

The Snake

Slithering, hissing

Tasting the air with its tongue

Swallows a mouse whole

The Golden Eagle

The golden eagle

Swooping down to catch a mouse

Feeds it to its young

The Sharks

A great white shark here

A grey reef shark over there

The lords of the sea

Provide a selection of musical instruments. Depending on the resources at your disposal, either invite the students to rehearse and perform their leitmotiv live, or record each using a camcorder or computer with a separate microphone and headphones. It helps if each student or small team takes turns to devise and record their leitmotiv in a quiet room.

Materials:
Musical instruments, a quiet room, sound recording equipment

(See **5.2 Recording and Editing Sound** for further technical advice.)

2.4 STORYTELLING

WORKSHEET: STORY WRITING

Teachers' note:

This is a simple and effective exercise to demonstrate how easy it is to construct a short story with a classic narrative structure.

Give each student pen and paper.

Ask them to write down the name of a character. Ask:

- Who is this character?
- Is s/he human, animal, alien, imaginary or a sentient object?
- Now think of a friend or enemy for this character. Again, what kind of life form is it?
- Think of a place where these two characters meet. It could be somewhere domestic and mundane, or exotic and imaginary. The choice is yours.
- Now, think of a problem, conflict or challenge that the two face together.
- Finally, describe how they overcome or resolve it.

At this stage the students should have a set of headings written down. Now invite them to flesh out their headings into one-page stories. They might consider which character is the hero and which the villain. What will we learn about each character through their actions? What happens as the two characters sort out the problem facing them? Characters express emotions through actions and words. The more they **do** rather than **say** the better.

The finished stories should include a beginning (which sets the stage, establishes the key characters and conflict). They should have a middle (in which the conflict or problem builds to a climax) and an ending (when the problem is resolved).

Many stories often have a black moment. This usually coincides with the climax, when almost everything seems lost and the hero seems to be doomed to failure.

Ask the students to read out their finished stories. Analyse the results and discuss if and how they conform to the classical storytelling form.

A good story should:

- have a clearly defined, single theme
- contain a well-developed plot
- have style: vivid word pictures, pleasing sounds and rhythm
- be driven by strong characters which come alive to the reader
- have dramatic appeal
- be appropriate to, and interest its intended audience

This is an excellent exercise for generating a script for a short animation. It works for any length of story, even a 60-word one suitable for a 20-second animation. If students are working in small teams, it can be a good idea to ask all the members of the team to write their own story, then build a hybrid version, incorporating the best ideas and characters.

Materials:
Pens and exercise books

WORKSHEET: ANALYSING STORY STRUCTURE

Teachers' note:
Ask your students to each choose a favourite animated film and identify its theme, genre, main characters and storyline. These headings will allow you to begin to see what the story involves. When you compare the different lists you may well see lots of similarities.

FILM TITLE

THEME

GENRE

MAIN CHARACTERS AND THEIR TYPES

STORYLINE:

BEGINNING
(Establishing the conflict)

MIDDLE
(Conflict builds to black moment)

END
(Resolution)

Now ask the students to repeat the exercise for an original story they would like to write themselves.

Materials:
Exercise books, pens

WORKSHEET: STORYTELLING WITH A VIDEO CAMERA

Teachers' note:

This exercise involves live action rather than animation. However, it is a wonderful warm-up activity to help students understand how to use a video camera and how to use basic film language to tell a simple story. The skills can then be applied to any genre.

The exercise has also been tried successfully in English lessons, to help inspire observational creative writing.

One group of students enact an everyday scenario, for example, waiting for the bus while chatting about events of the day. They do not 'act to camera'. It's good to select an unstructured, ongoing situation in which the actors improvise.

Alternatively, choose another school activity as your subject, for example, a sporting event, a cookery class, etc.

Camera/director team's task:

Tell a story on camera about what you see. Limit your choices to the visual realm, rather than attempting to record specific conversations. You won't be editing the film, so shoot in the order you want to view the finished sequence.

Hints and tips:

Consider using close-ups and medium static shots to isolate important details. Consider which details to choose and why. If you decide to use zooms, pans or tilts, how do they shift focus for the audience? What is their dramatic intent? What do they tell us about the subject that a static shot can't?

Consider establishing the situation with one or more wide shots. How does each shot help to unfold the story? How might you keep your audience interested by mixing different camera angles and shot types?

Think about the information you wish to include and what can be ignored.

Review the footage:

In discussing the end result, ask these questions:

- Has your sequence combined to tell a coherent story?
- How might an audience interpret what they see?
- Have you applied bias through your shot selection process?
- If so, what point of view have you articulated?

Materials:

Data projector, whiteboard or screen and sound (to review the video), video camera and tape

WORKSHEET: SCRIPT WRITING FOR ANIMATION

Teachers' note:

The script is where everything starts. It's a roadmap, a plan, a guide, a source to be inspired by. Typically, before anything else happens in producing a film project of any scale an idea is written down, first as a brief outline or treatment, then as a more detailed breakdown of the story and finally as a script which everybody works from.

A script is a key document involved in the creation of any film. A good script should describe action with just enough detail, but not too much, to inspire amazing images. A script will give you an idea of structure, character, action and tone. The script can be supplemented by your storyboard.

Don't write camera movements or compositions into the script, just use it for story structure, dialogue, action and events. (Compositions can be better described in the storyboard.)

In most cases there will be a sense of a beginning, middle and an end. Establish a situation, complicate it, resolve it. Invite us into your world and make us curious about what is going to happen. Send us, the viewers on a journey we did not expect to go on. Shake us up with a 'black' moment, just before it all ends with a solution.

Remember that animation can subvert and amplify reality.

Some students find that writing their ideas in script form comes easily to them. Some prefer to think in drawings and storyboards, others are equally comfortable doing both. There is no one right way to develop a story idea. Most animation productions are the result of teamwork, so a key task is to delegate roles according to each member's particular talents.

A popular approach is to begin with a text-only script, then develop the storyboard from that, adding the appropriate lines of script under each storyboard frame.

An effective script-writing exercise is to give each student a short story of one to three paragraphs. Ask the students to adapt the story into a script, adopting the same format as the example in the Headless Smuggler handout.

The source of the original story is included in the **Resources** below. Students might also like to watch the finished film that was made from the Headless Smuggler script, also available on the companion website.

Materials:
Exercise books, pens

Resources:
Handout: The Headless Smuggler Script 🖱

Video: The Headless Smuggler 🖱

Publication: Norfolk: A Ghost Hunter's Guide, Neil R Storey, Countryside Books 2007. Available on Amazon here: http://www.amazon.co.uk/Norfolk-Ghosthunters-Guide/dp/1846740592/ ref=sr_1_1?ie=UTF8&s=books&qid=1289837062&sr=8–1

HANDOUT: THE HEADLESS SMUGGLER SCRIPT EXAMPLE

Action Describe the action and the setting.	Sound Narration, dialogue, sound effects, music, length. (Narration is 3 words per second.)
Shot 1: Waves crashing on the shore	Narrator: It was the 4 March 1793 and the grey sea of the North Norfolk coast was splashing against the grey rocks of Happisburgh beach. Loud shouts and laughter came from the Hill House pub. Length: 15 secs
Shot 2: Outside the Pub. At the door of the pub. Landlord is dragging two drunks out the door.	Landlord: Be off with you, you scoundrels. There'll be no more rum for you tonight. Bill: It's all right Mr Screwloose. We wont be wanting no more rum from this pub. We can get much more bootiful rum from the Pig and Whistle. Joseph: Oi . . . landlord. Why you got such a long face? Was your mother a horse? Neigh . . . neigh. . . . Length: 20 secs
Shot 3: Walking down the lane, the two drunks wobble along the hedgerow.	Bill: We had better hurry up, it's 2 am. Stupid old landlord . . . Joseph: Yeah- he's a horseface, horseface, horseface. . . .
Shot 4: Bill, looking puzzled.	Bill: Oi . . . look at that man with a sack on his back. Length: 4 secs
Shot 5: A grey form with a lump on his back moves towards the camera.	Bill: SACK BACK SACK BACK SACK BACK! Length: 3 secs
Shot 6: Joseph and Bill look at each other, baffled and a little scared.	Joseph: Oy . . . come back here, sackback. We wanna talk to you! Length: 3 secs
Shot 7: The glowing light moves closer, gradually revealing itself as a lantern, held by a shadowy figure without a head or arms. The figure moves up to the village well and drops into it.	Bill: Oh my god . . . it's not a sack . . . it's his head . . . and he's . . . he's gone down the well! Length: 5 secs
Shot 8: Bill and Joseph turn in their heels, and rush back to the pub.	Joseph: Help . . . help, there's a ghost! Run for your life! Length: 10 secs

(Continued)

Shot 9: Joseph is pounding on the door of the pub. Landlord opens door a crack, looks out and slams it shut. He opens it again and steps out.	Joseph: Horseface, horseface . . . open up! There's a goul out here. There's a headless man out here! I mean it! Let us in! Length: 7 secs
Shot 10: landlord looks at Joseph. Bill catches up, out of breath.	Landlord: You're shaking. You look as if you've seen a ghost! Joseph: I have. I have. It's got no legs and . . . and . . . I could see right through him! Bill: It's true . . . It's true. And its head is dangling down its back on a thin strip of skin. Landlord: I don't believe a word. There's no such thing as ghosts. Length: 20 secs
Shot 11: Tom is lowered down the well on a rope. He pulls up two parcels.	Narrator: Well, well well. The next day Joseph, Billy, Mr Screwloose and his son Tom went to Happisburgh well. Young Tom climbed down the well and found two big parcels. Length: 10 secs
Shot 12: The parcel contents	Narrator: The parcels were full of bloody body parts, including a head dangling on a strip of skin. Length: 6 secs
Shot 13: Close up of magnifying glass in hand, looking at suspicious marks.	Narrator: The gang searched the village for clues. Length: 3 secs
Shot 14: A finger poking at the blood.	Narrator: They walked to Cart Gap and discovered a pool of congealed blood near the sand dunes. Length: 9 secs
Shot 15: Hand pulling a pistol out of the sand.	Narrator: Tom found a pistol half buried in the sand, where the murder had taken place. Length: 5 secs
Shot 16: Spectral lights hovering over the landcape. Fade to black.	Narrator: To this day, locals still see a strange glowing spectre floating along the hedgerows on wild winter nights. Perhaps the ghost is still looking for his killers! Length: 10 secs

(Based on a script by George Fenn)

WORKSHEET: STORYBOARDING

Teachers' note:

Almost every animation starts with a storyboard. When working in animation on a professional level it is vital, as a storyboard artist, to produce a crystal clear storyboard that you can pass on to the animation artists.

To draw an effective storyboard, students will need a grasp of film language, and many of the preceding exercises will act as a grounding for this.

Download and print the handout: Storyboard Template. A4 is generally too small a format to include all the information a storyboard needs. It's better to scale up the template to A3 or A2, using it as a guide. Note the three boxes. The larger boxes will contain the key frame drawings for each shot. The **Action** box will contain a description of the visible action within the shot. This is a guide for the animator and should not be confused with the narration. (It is the same as the Action column in the handout: The Headless Smuggler Script Example.) The **SFX, Narration** box will contain the narration and/or dialogue and sound effects, once again following the format of the script example. You will immediately see why, for more complex projects, it might well be tidier to write out the **Action** and **SFX, Narration** as a separate script. If so, make sure the shot numbers tally between script and storyboard.

For a preliminary exercise in storyboarding, download the self-explanatory handout: Storyboard Sequencing. Students can then watch the final film that was made from the storyboard, to see if they sequenced the shots in the same way as the artist.

Follow this up by asking the students to write a six-frame storyboard for a story of their own.

You might also wish to download the handout: Storyboard Example: A Decent Excuse. A study of this will help students to understand the purpose of a storyboard before they draw their own. It follows a simpler format to the template, combining key frame drawings of each shot with action and shot timing only.

Hints and tips:

Beginners tend to draw their stories from a single point of view, often a static wide angle shot from directly in front of the characters. Encourage students to use a mix of wide, medium- and close-up shots, thinking about their choices in relation to their storytelling.

Explain the concept of a jump cut. If two wide angle shots are placed side by side on the storyboard, each with the same framing, there will be a jump cut in the action between the end of the first shot and beginning of the second. To avoid this, make sure to change the composition between shots.

Often, students will want a narrator to tell the story and/or add dialogue. Make sure the narration fits the intended shot length. The rule of thumb is—we say three words per second on average.

Don't worry about drawing skills. Stick men and simple line drawings are fine.

The important point is that students use film language creatively and visualize how they want each shot to look before they start work at the animation rostrum.

Don't build camera movements, including zooms, pans and tilts into the storyboard. The technology available in the classroom makes the smooth animation of camera movement very difficult. Students often attempt animated zooms, but the results can be very jerky. It's much better that students solve the problems of how to tell their story through the use of close-up, medium and wide static shots.

Encourage students to put in as much information as they can on their storyboards, so that if they hand them on to other animators, they will be able to understand them without having to ask questions.

Materials:
Sketchbooks, pens, pencils, rulers, erasers

Resources:
Handout: Storyboard Template:

Handout: Storyboard Sequencing: 🖱

Handout: A Decent Excuse Storyboard: 🖱

Video clip: A Decent Excuse by Julian Frank: 🖱

WORKSHEET: STORYBOARDING AN ANIMATED HAIKU

Teachers' note:

Haiku is a short form of poetry that developed in Japan from about 400 years ago. The style reached a peak in the first half of the Edo period (1600–1868), when a poet named Masuo Basho wrote distinctive verses on his journeys around the country describing the seasons and the scenery of the places he visited.

A Haiku is a short verse of 17 syllables and it is made up of 3 lines. The first line usually has 5 syllables, the second has 7 and the third, last line has 5 syllables again.

Haiku use simple expressions in ways that allow deeply felt emotions and a sense of discovery. Traditionally, a Haiku must have a word that is identified with a particular season.

The popularity of Haiku has spread beyond Japan to Europe, North America, United States, Africa and China. The following are English translations of Haiku by Matsuo Basho.

The Haiku lends itself ideally to animation, because of its brevity, and use of powerful word images. When students plan storyboards to complement their written Haiku, remind them that the visuals need not necessarily depict exactly what the words describe. It can be more challenging to consider how else to extend the word picture, using detail, mood, gesture, etc.

A cat sleeps in the afternoon sun while the flowers grow	The autumn wind is blowing but the chestnut burs are green	Someone is living there smoke leaks through the wall in the spring rain
A crazy old man by the shore of the river waits there patiently	Darkness everyday and until my time is through I will wait for you	The young dancing girl moving fast, twisting, turning not knowing I watch

Each example above could be used as the basis for a one, two or three-shot storyboard. Invite your students to write their own haiku.

Materials:
Sketchbooks, pens, pencils, erasers

Resources:
Internet links: A history: http://en.wikipedia.org/wiki/Haiku

Start Writing Haiku:
  http://www.cc.matsuyama-u.ac.jp/~shiki/Start-Writing.html

Video clip: Silence Haiku Animation by Ampur0909
  http://www.youtube.com/watch?v=M2aZeyyi098&playnext=1&list=
  PL6061D0AEDE121AB2&index=6

PART THREE: ANIMATION STYLES

3.1 PIXILATION

WORKSHEET: ANIMATED PORTRAITS

Teachers' note:

Norman McLaren coined the term pixilation for the stop-motion animation technique that involves shooting, one frame at a time, characters or objects whose movements are controlled entirely by the filmmaker. These objects can range from fruit to toys to sticks and stones . . . even the human body or face. Live actors can be used as a frame-by-frame subject in an animated film, by repeatedly posing while one frame is taken and changing pose slightly before the next frame. The actor becomes a kind of living stop-motion puppet. The word pixilation comes from the use of the word pixie as if to suggest the image and action has been affected by otherworldly forces!

In this activity, students will create animated portraits of themselves, by recording a sequence of still images, which together create the illusion of a surreal dance. Invite them to use props if they wish, such as trees in the landscape or chairs and tables in the room. Encourage them to think about creating impossible body movements, gestures and expressions.

Here are some variations on a theme:

Anti-gravity

Ask the actor/s to jump into the air. Capture each frame at the highest point of the jump. Repeat with variations.

Ice skating

The actors slide in procession across the frame by animating a shot, moving forwards a foot, freezing a gesture, animating, etc. etc. until they pass through the picture.

Crazy faces

Set up the camera in front of a chair. Form an orderly queue of actors. Each actor sits on the chair in turn and pulls a face, while the expression is captured in two frames. Try to get all the faces to line up in the composition.

Hints and tips

Create a studio space using a backdrop curtain and studio lights, if available. Lock the camera in a fixed position on tripod. Alternatively, make creative use of an outdoor location.

Try to plan a sequence ahead of time, rather than simply improvising. Try to imagine how to break down the desired effect into single frame poses.

Materials:

A video camera with a stop-motion recording mode, or a camera linked to a laptop, running stop-frame capture software (see **Resources** section, p. 122 for further details), lights if available

Resources:
Video:

Pixilation

Big Bang Big Boom by Blu (a combination of wall painted animation and pixilation) http://vimeo.com/13085676

Norman McLaren's *A Chairy Tale* (see Into Animation, BFI VHS compilation and teaching guide on CD) http://filmstore.bfi.org.uk/acatalog/info_3963.html

Pixilation Short Film by Dustball and André Nguyen Spin on http://www.youtube.com/watch?v=pbMnOrq50iA

Pixilation Music Video by Sebastián Baptista Fuerte on http://www.youtube.com/watch?v=MXALzTinIHE

Sorry I'm Late by Tomas Mankovsky *on* http://www.bbc.co.uk/filmnetwork/films/p006x5jz

Music Videos (on You Tube):

Road to Nowhere by Talking Heads

The Hardest Button to Button by The White Stripes

Sledgehammer by Peter Gabriel

Point of No Return by Nu Shooz

Heard 'Em Say by Kanye West

Hello Again by The Cars

Shopping Trolley by Beth Orton

The Box by Orbital

The End of the World by The Cure

Strawberry Swing by Coldplay

Animating the human body

WORKSHEET: ANIMATION IN THE LANDSCAPE

Teachers' note:

Working in small teams, invite students to make short animations, inspired by the immediate landscape surrounding the school. The theme can be either abstract, narrative based or kinaesthetic (i.e. exploring the aesthetics of choreographed movement).

They may explore any of the following techniques:

Timelapse

Stop-frame animation can be used to accelerate the perception of time passing, making clouds rush across the sky, spring flowers open their petals or people dash their dogs around the park!

Pixilation

Found objects, plasticine characters, 2D art etc. can be brought to life, and interact with their surroundings using animation.

Choreography of the human form

Animated facial expressions, body gestures and movements can take on surreal, dramatic or humorous qualities. Think about working with props like hats, fancy dress, chairs etc.

Single frame montage

Kinetic textures and serial patterns can be generated by shooting sequences of stills, frame by frame. A brick wall can be transformed into a vibrating, abstracted sea of shape and colour, by filming four bricks per frame!

Materials:

Each team will need a video camera, tripod and laptop on which to capture images frame by frame. Teams should prepare storyboards or outlines of their idea and think about both the imagery and sound they will need.

Resources:

Video: Window Pane by Jenny McCormack. A pixilated self-portrait.
   http://www.videoart.net/home/Artists/VideoPage.cfm?Artist_
   ID=1236&ArtWork_ID=1381&Player_ID=10

Singing The Horizon by Martin Sercombe and Sianed Jones

A landscape film using time-lapse and other techniques.

The Listening Place by Martin Sercombe

A painterly vision of a working day in the life of Cambridge market, using time-lapse.

Both films can be seen together here:
http://blip.tv/shinyshabazz/singing-the-horizon-and-the-listening-place-476092

WORKSHEET: TALKING OBJECTS

Teachers' note:
Ask your students to devise a character from a selection of objects, or a single item such as an apple. They should decide if their character works best in 2D or 3D. An apple would need a table-top set, with the animation camera looking across to it. A dancing pair of scissors or 'button man' would animate in a 2D plane, with the camera set above, looking down.

Ask each animator to make the character perform a simple gesture, dance or change of expression. Two seconds of animation will suffice per gesture.

Next they should each imagine the sound the character is making. Ask the students to perform this sound live as they playback the animation on the computer screen. Use voice to improvise sound effects or use a musical instrument.

They can then record these sounds and edit them to the animations using any preferred software package.

Extension work:
Storyboard a 20-second animation involving the characters and ideas suggested by the previous activity. Use the standard storyboard template, and draw the story in six shots. Add narration, dialogue and/or effects.

Materials:
A 2D or 3D animation rostrum per student or small group, a collection of found objects such as fruit, mechanical objects, leaves, shells, feathers, buttons or scissors, musical instruments, sound recording equipment.

Resources:
Video: the work of Jan Svankmajer, especially Dimensions of Dialogue:
   http://video.google.com/videoplay?docid=5053516656925914770#

3.2 PLASTICINE MODEL ANIMATION

WORKSHEET: METAMORPHOSIS

Teachers' note:
Plasticine animation is a firm favourite with all ages for many reasons. It is an ideal medium for animation, because the models can be articulated easily in small incremental movements. Plasticine is also very malleable; so all kinds of transformations and metamorphoses are possible. It comes in a wide variety of colours, including ranges of flesh tones. Most importantly, it is cheap if ordered from an educational supplier.

"It's the beauty of plasticine animation that you can make (characters) very human by manipulating them frame by frame." Nick Park.

Invite students to explain the meaning of the word metamorphosis. Talk about examples from the animal and botanical world, or help the pupils to develop their own imaginary ideas. Have each student form a plasticine ball. Talk about shapes and forms. Ask the pupils what the ball could change into. When they have decided on their transformation, ask them to plan how they will achieve this in several stages. Ask them to animate the transformations and play them back. Discuss the results.

Hints and tips:
Work the plasticine well to warm it up. It is often difficult to model straight out of the packet. Most models can be built from the basic shapes of the ball and sausage. Both can be easily rolled out with hands on a flat surface. Cover tables with newspaper before work begins, as plasticine is hard to clean from table tops. Take care not to drop plasticine on carpets. It can be very difficult to remove!

Materials:
Plasticine, newspaper, 3D animation rostrums and lights

Resources:

Video: Black Shuck 🖱

Why Did the Chicken Cross the Road? 🖱

Little Red Riding Hood 🖱

Screen Play directed by Barry Purves:
  http://www.barrypurves.com/Films/Screenplay/index.html

Chicken Run directed by Nick Park and Peter Lord Trailer:
  http://www.metacafe.com/watch/3014083/chicken_run_trailer/

Creature Comforts, directed by Nick Park on
  http://www.atomfilms.com/film/creature_comforts.jsp

Frogland directed by Wladislaw Starewicz
  http://www.youtube.com/watch?v=oPmLi3zYaE8

Article about the work of Nick Park:
  http://news.bbc.co.uk/1/hi/entertainment/2313157.stm

Animate Clay website about 3D stop motion:
  http://www.animateclay.com/

Aardman Animation's website is a good place to start:
  http://www.aardman.com

Model making

WORKSHEET: TWO CHARACTERS

Teachers' note:
Working in teams of two, ask each student to devise a plasticine character. It can be human, animal or alien! Ask each pair of students to devise a one-shot interaction between the two characters. It might be a dance, a greeting, a stroll in the park, a swim in the sea. Invite them to animate this. Five seconds should be plenty. Review, discuss and reshoot if necessary.

Extension work:
Use these two characters as the basis for a short story. Ask each team to draw up a six-shot storyboard, then shoot the animation. The story is likely to require at least one set, which can be prepared using a sheet of sugar paper and pastels, or any other available art materials.

Hints and tips:
Encourage pupils to test the stability of their models as they make them, by standing them upright. Beginners often make their characters top heavy, so they collapse easily. This can be frustrating when they come to animate them. Big feet, stocky legs and smaller heads are the order of the day. If pupils are creating animals or imaginary creatures, encourage them to give them expressive features, limbs, tentacles etc. These can all be used to give the character life and expression as they are articulated in different ways.

Materials:
Plasticine, sugar paper, pastels, 3D animation rostrums and lights

Resources:
See previous worksheet.

Making a plasticine character

3.3 CUT-OUT ANIMATION

WORKSHEET: CUT-OUT FIGURES

Teachers' note:

Cut-out animation is a technique for producing animations using flat characters, props and backgrounds cut from materials such as paper, card, stiff fabric or even photographs. Cut-outs are top lit to emphasize colours, textures, etc. Silhouette cut-out animation is backlit and hence the figure appears solid. Silhouette-style cut-outs are also discussed in the **Shadow Puppetry** section that follows.

Working in teams of two, ask each student to devise a cut-out character. It is important that the character is designed to use the limitations of a 2D world to maximum advantage. It is easy to make a fish float and swim, or a human figure walk in one direction. It's impossible for a character to walk towards the camera!

Consider which parts of the character will have independent movement, if any. If the character has articulated limbs, they need to be drawn and cut out separately, with an overlap to accommodate a joint. The joints can be made using BluTak or paper fasteners.

Ask each pair of students to devise a short interplay between the two characters. Animate, review, discuss and reshoot if necessary.

Extension work:

Use these two characters as the basis for a short story. Ask each team to draw up a six-shot storyboard, then shoot the animation. The story is likely to require at least one background, which can be prepared using a sheet of sugar paper and pastels, or any other available art materials.

Another technique to consider is replacement animation. This involves making a sequence of cut-out shapes then cycling them to create the illusion of movement. This technique can allow a bird to fly, a face to change from a frown to a smile or a seedling to grow into a mature tree.

The following activity uses replacement animation, and might be useful as an initial warm-up exercise for younger students:

Ask each student to draw just the outline of a head onto thin white card and cut it out. Then draw the following items on the cardboard and cut them out:

- Four sets of eyes from wide open to nearly closed
- Six mouths showing the sounds a e i o u and very wide open
- Four sets of odd-shaped ears
- Four sets of eyebrows
- Four hair styles
- Four different hats

Make up different faces with these cut-outs. Pull faces in a mirror to get some ideas. Another way to make cut-outs is to stick magazine photos onto cardboard and cut around them. You can make pictures larger by using a photocopier. You can reverse them by tracing over the original then tracing over the back of the tracing paper.

Next animate each face by mix and matching different combinations of features.

Materials:
Thin card in various colours, glue sticks, scissors, sugar paper, pastels or crayons, BluTak and/or paper fasteners, 2D animation rostrums and lights.

Resources:
Video: Eco Monkey

Lotte Reiniger's animated feature The Adventures of Prince Achmed (extract) http://www.youtube.com/watch?v=25SP4ftxklg

Terry Gilliam's animated sequences for the Monty Python TV series and films: http://www.youtube.com/watch?v=Tq37WSg9ESg

Yuri Nortstein's film *The Fox and the Hare*, 1973. http://www.youtube.com/watch?v=Vo4ccROH55E

Chris Marker's photo collage film La Jetee. http://www.youtube.com/watch?v=ClvTYd4XnEc

South Park: Bigger, Longer & Uncut uses computer animation to imitate the look of cut-out animation. http://smotri.com/video/view/?id=v10574062841

The closing credits of the film of Lemony Snicket's A Series of Unfortunate Events mimics the style of cut-out animation, though sophisticated animation software was used.

The TV series of Lauren Child's Charlie and Lola. http://www.charlieandlola.com/

Angela Anaconda combines black-and-white photographs with cut-out-style CGI animation. http://www.angelaa.com/

Cut-out Pro's Stickman software can be used to create cut-out-style animations. http://www.cutoutpro.com

The Museum of Childhood: This webpage offers great resources. Here you can find classroom friendly instructions and templates to make silhouettes, cut-outs, jumping jacks and more. http://www.vam.ac.uk/moc/kids/things_to_make/jumping_jack/index.html

Cut-out fairytale animation

3.4 SHADOW PUPPETRY

WORKSHEET: SHADOW PUPPET ANIMATION

Teachers' note:

Shadows have always fascinated people. Shadow puppets originated in China and records show that puppets were first demonstrated around 2,000 years ago. Putting hands and fingers into a beam of light can turn them into mysterious animal heads or monsters. A whole world can be conjured in moments by cutting simple shapes out of black card and placing them on an overhead projector.

Coloured cellophane or acetate is a quick and effective way to add colour. Figures made of black card can have coloured eyes or decoration added by cutting holes in the card, and glueing on coloured gel over the holes. Figures can be jointed to allow them to move and perform gestures.

A still from Dreams by Holly Sandiford. See the companion website.

Students can also experiment with painting effects by using glass paints or marker pens on clear acetate sheets. These can be cut up to make moveable puppets or used for backgrounds. All kinds of fabrics, translucent materials and found objects can be used to create interesting textures, when placed on the projector.

Invite the students to cut out shapes like a sun, a hill and trees then place the pieces on the overhead projector. These can be used as your background.

It helps if the background is quite simple. Often strips of coloured cellophane to depict sky and grass work the best.

Next, ask the students to make characters using thin black card or acetate sheets and marker pens. Remind them to keep each puppet small in size. It must fit on the overhead projector.

If the students want to tell their stories live they will need to add handles to each puppet so they can be moved in real time. (Pipe cleaners or modelling sticks are ideal for this.) Ask them to create short dialogue-based scenes using the puppets, around a given theme.

Extension work:
The live improvisation is a good introduction to the medium. It can then be developed into an animation, by adding a video camera framed on the screen and linked to single frame capture software.

This opens up a further set of creative possibilities. Puppets no longer need handles to articulate them. All kinds of additional effects can be explored via stop motion. Animation and live action can be combined in the same project, if desired.

Materials (some of these are optional):
Black card, an overhead projector and white wall or screen, glue, scissors, paper fasteners or BluTak, coloured cellophane, fabric scraps, clear acetate sheets, glass paints, pipe cleaners, modelling sticks, permanent marker pens, camera and tripod linked to stop-motion software.

Resources:

Video: Dreams by Holly Sandiford 🖱

Shadow animation:
   http://www.gagneint.com/Final%20site/insanelytwisted.com/main.htm

http://www.youtube.com/watch?v=Meg_gZXcF44

3.5 DRAWN ANIMATION

WORSHEET: SIMPLE MOVEMENT CYCLES

Teachers' note:

Hand-drawn animation is perhaps the style we are most familiar with, through the work of Walt Disney. If approached in this traditional way, it can be one of the most labour intensive and technically demanding of animation styles. However, short hand-drawn animations are easily achieved in the classroom. Make your figures simple and not too detailed. Perhaps start by doing a stick figure flick book. Start with line drawings, and focus on making simple movements and transformations work, before adding colour, shade, texture etc.

For these exercises, each student will need thin A4 photocopy paper or tracing paper, soft pencils and a ring binder with the standard 2D mechanism. They will also need one of the two handouts: Hand-Drawn Animation in 4:3 Aspect Ratio or 16:9 aspect ratio, depending on the camera you are using (4:3 is for standard, 16:9 is widescreen). The handout shows where the drawings can be placed on the page and still be seen on camera, without including the page edge. Note the black circles. This is where holes should be punched, so the sheets can be inserted in the ring binder, which will provide a means of registration. If you don't have ring binders to hand, the sheets can be registered by placing them on cards with A4 guide marks at each corner. Another option is to order peg bars from an animation supplier.

It's very important that students can see their previous drawing when they place the next sheet over it. They can use a light box or window to help if necessary.

Explain the technique of Inbetweening: Inbetweening is producing intermediate drawings in between the key drawings, which break the movement into stop-frame increments. Key frames are significant poses in a character's action, for example, the first and the last position of a jump. Inbetweens are all of the drawings needed between the key frames to create the illusion of smooth movement.

Ask them to try the following:

Draw a pendulum swing

Draw the path for a swinging pendulum using 7 drawings. Remind them that the pendulum swings more slowly at the extents of its swing. Ask them to plan how they will show this.

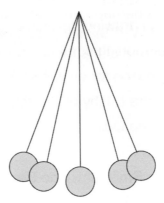

Bouncing ball

Draw the path of action of a bouncing ball in 12 drawings. Again, remind them to focus on the changing speed of the ball, and to show this in the drawings. Ask them to give the ball some squash as it hits the ground. They should draw the key frames first, then the inbetweens.

Metamorphosis

Transform one simple object into another and then back again.

Simple movements cycles (on the companion website) shows a range of very simple-drawn exercises to warm up with. They were made by a class of 7-year-olds, and explore bounce, additive animation and metamorphosis techniques.

Materials:

Thin white A4 paper or tracing paper, soft pencils, hole punch, ring binders, 2D animation rostrum, lights, lightbox if available

Resources:

Handouts: Hand-Drawn Animation Standard or
    Widescreen: ᠕🖱

Video: Simple Movement Cycles: 🖱

    Drawn Animation 🖱

    Simple Movement Cycles 🖱

    A Decent Excuse 🖱

    Tolerance 🖱

    Bubbletown 🖱

Web-based introduction to drawing cartoons:

    http://www.followmecartooning.com/

Films on DVD (Check Amazon for availability):

    Fast Spin Fling by Sandra Ensby of Sherbet Productions

    Girls Night Out by Joanna Quinn

    The Snowman by Varga Films

    El Caminante by Debra Smith of Rhino Films Ltd.

    Gertie the Dinosaur by Winsor McCay

    Bambi, Aladdin et al. by Walt Disney Studio

    The Man Who Planted Trees by Frederic Back

    Spirited Away by Hayao Miyazaki

Drawing Expressions

WORKSHEET: DRAWING KEY FRAMES AND INBETWEENS

Teachers' note:

This is an excellent exercise for students of drawn animation. Invite one student to perform a sequence of movements in front of the group, for example, sitting down, bowling, karate or ballet. Get the performer to freeze the action at the start, middle and end.

Ask the class to draw the three key frames of the movement performed.

If students lack confidence in their drawing skills, encourage them to work in stick man style. This can help them to focus on analysing movement, rather than drawing technique.

Actions:

- Kicking a football
- Walking
- Picking up a cup and drinking from it
- Hammering a nail
- Putting on a hat
- Being frightened by a ghost
- A cowboy with a lasso trying to catch cattle
- A dog scratching his ear

Invite the performers to think up different actions. If they are more complex, up to six key frames may be needed. The class might wish to develop their favourite movements into short animated cycles by filling in the inbetweens.

Materials:

Thin white A4 paper or tracing paper, soft pencils, hole punch, ring binders, 2D animation rostrum, lights, lightbox if available

Resources:

Handouts: Hand-Drawn Animation Standard or
   Widescreen:

Video clips: see previous worksheet.

WORKSHEET: LIP SYNC

Teachers' note:

Making a speaking character's lip movements syncronize with their speech track is an advanced technique and a full description of the methods used in the industry is beyond the scope of this toolkit. However, this exercise is a simple and fun way to help students with their drawing and observation skills. Some may find they need to use lip sync in more advanced projects at a later stage. If so, Toon Boom Studio, the drawn animation software package, has a system for matching key framed mouth shapes to a dialogue audio track.

Materials:

Pencils, mirrors

Resources:

Handouts: Lip Sync and Mouth Shapes

WORKSHEET: DIGITAL DRAWN ANIMATION

Teachers' note:

Digital drawn animation requires a drawing tablet linked to a suitable software package on a desktop or laptop computer. To equip an entire classroom or IT suite with these is a major investment. However, it is well worth considering providing a few workstations, so that small groups of students can explore this exciting approach to the medium. The following is an example of an extended class-based project, which could be used as a model for similar work in your school.

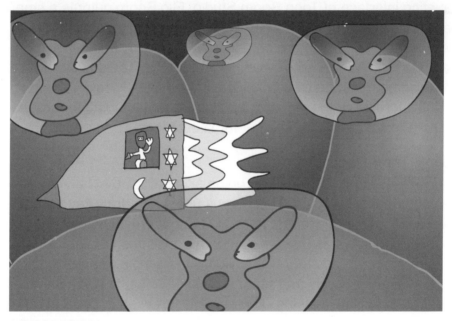

A Still from Bubbletown

Bubbletown

Bubbletown is a drawn sci-fi animation, made by a group of 12 seven-year-olds from Dowson First School in Norwich. To master the basic principles of drawn animation, the students began with the warm-up exercises on pp. 27–29. They then storyboarded the tale in 12 scenes, working in teams of two. They fitted each scene to a couplet from their song, whose lyrics tell the story. The students then sang the song to a pre-recorded backing track. The shots were exported as avi files to Premiere Pro, where they were cut to the final mix of the song. The rough cut was projected on a whiteboard, so the team could share in the editing process. The project took 11 mornings of contact time, followed by five days of studio-based post-production. It was supported by First Light Films, which provides film production funding for young people in the United Kingdom.

Materials:

Each team of two worked with a drawing tablet, connected to a laptop. They used Toon Boom Studio, a professional 2D drawn animation package costing around £100 for an educational licence. A cheaper alternative, Flip Boom, designed for students, is available from the same company, for around £25. We strongly recommend Flip Boom for beginners, as it greatly simplifies the somewhat daunting interface of Toon Boom Studio. Flip Boom outputs a smaller frame size than that required for DVD production, but is fine for web-based work. If you are on a tight budget, look at the Wacom Bamboo One A6 graphics tablet, for about £35. The small drawing area can be frustrating, so consider an A4 Aiptek Media Tablet 14000U for £94 or the industry leading Wacom Intuos 3 for around £300. (Please check the internet for latest models and prices.)

Using Toon Boom Studio

Toon Boom Studio provides an onion skin facility, that is, virtual tracing paper to draw on. This means users can draw key frames, then add in the inbetweens, referring to both previous and subsequent drawings to create smooth transitions between key frames. Much of the story was built around simple, repeating cycles, such as waving hands and pulsing rocket flames, to minimize the need for extensive drawing. The students drew each cycle in outline first, checked the movement worked, then filled in the shapes with colour. Characters can then be placed on virtual tracks, allowing the computer to work out the desired movements in 3D space. The software also allows users to paint backgrounds separately to the moving subjects, which greatly simplifies the drawing process.

Resources:

Video: Bubbletown and Simple Movement Cycles

Toon Boom website: http://www.toonboom.com/

3.6 MACHINIMA

WORKSHEET: MAKING MACHINIMA IN SECOND LIFE

Teachers' note:

Machinima (mah-sheen-eh-mah) is filmmaking within a real-time, 3D virtual environment. Machinima is real-world filmmaking techniques applied within an interactive virtual space where characters and events can be either controlled by humans, scripts or artificial intelligence. It is debatable whether or not this can be defined as a style of animation, as the movement of characters and objects occurs in real time, driven by the controls provided by the software interface.

Filming machinima in Second Life

The process of making a film in a virtual world is perhaps too complex to attempt as a conventional classroom activity. A comprehensive how to guide is well beyond the scope of this book. However, it is a very exciting medium for small groups of enthused students, willing and able to master the software tools involved. It challenges the very concepts of 'teacher' and 'classroom', as students from all over the world can meet together in a virtual environment, exchange ideas and work as a production team. As such, it is also a significant peer education model.

The Airship Hindenburg

We have included this film on the companion website as an example of a model of working you might wish to support at your school. The Airship Hindenburg was made by 12- to 16-year-olds in Schome Park, a secure island within Teen Second Life. Residents of Schome Park each have an 'avatar', a 3D representation of themselves which can then interact with others, and the world they inhabit. Second Life has a highly sophisticated software interface, allowing users enormous creative freedom to build the 3D world around them, as well as live within it. This also interfaces with the tools needed to film events in world, which makes it ideal for machinima production.

Materials and software:

Students will need to first master the Second Life viewer (software interface), which is a free download for PCs or Macs. Extensive tutorials are available on the website. They will then need a plug-in to capture in world activity as avi video files. The best PC tool is Auto Screen Recorder 3 (approx. £50 per licence). A cheaper PC option is Fraps (approx. £20 per licence). Macintosh users can use Snapz Pro X (approx. £35). Please check the internet for latest versions and prices.

When they have captured their avi or mov files, they can import them into an editing software package. It is advisable to capture the files at the highest resolution the computer will allow, then downsample them to standard video files if necessary.

The finished edit can then be published on the internet. An excellent free software package to encode video files for the web is Super C. For files which can also be streamed in Second Life, use these settings: Output file: mov Video Codec: H.264/AAC Video Size: 853 x 480 pixels. Aspect Ratio: 16:9 Frames per Sec: 25 Video Bitrate: 768 kb per sec Audio Channels: 2 Audio Bitrate: 128 kb per sec. Pixel Aspect 1:1 For web publishing use mp4 rather than mov as your output file, for better image quality at this compression.

Resources:
Video: The Airship Hindenburg:

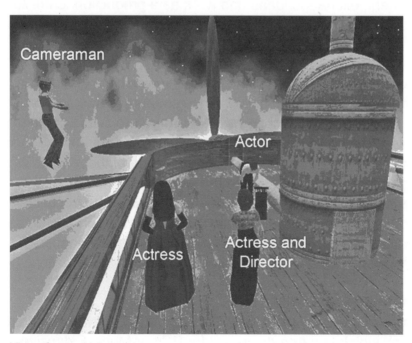

View of a machinima set

WORKSHEET: USING CRAZY TALK

Teachers' note:

Crazy Talk is a useful add-on tool for machinima filmmakers. Crazy Talk lets you bring still images of human or animal faces to life by automatically synchronizing lip movements to spoken dialogue or sung vocals. It will even animate facial expressions.

Students can create a music video of their own in under 10 minutes. Using the audio from a favourite song and Crazy Talk, anyone can become a music video director instantly. It can also be used to give machinima-based avatars the power of lip-synched speech.

The following is a product summary provided by the company:

Main features:

1. **Turn images into talking videos:**
    - Create 3D talking characters from any photo or image.
    - Easy tools to adjust eyes, lips, mouth and teeth.
    - Add automatic facial expressions and face morph effects.

2. **Makes images talk with voices and text:**
    - Automatic **lip-sync** animation performance from any **audio** or **typed text**.
    - Apply any instant animated **emotions** and **gestures**.
    - Add animated **SFX** for fun character disguises.

3. **Turn human and non-human images into talking avatars:**
    - Import images for custom teeth and eyes from teeth and eyes library.
    - Nine customizable character styles to match a variety of characters, from human to non-human such as cartoon, animal, machine and more.

4. **Edit the facial expression:**
    - Use a mouse or a handheld device to puppet character animation in real-time.

- Use puppet profiles for instant facial expression presets.
- Select attitudes matching various puppet personalities.

5.   **Flexible media output:**

Flash

Youtube

HD

MPEG-4

NTSC

PAL

Resources:
http://www.reallusion.com/crazytalk/

WORKSHEET: USING MOVIESTORM FOR MACHINIMA

Teachers' note:

Moviestorm is an alternative, software-based system for making machinima-style films, without the need to master Second Life and its related capture tools. Again, a step by step guide to using Moviestorm is outside the scope of this toolkit. We have included this description for the benefit of more advanced students interested in learning the skills involved outside the classroom context.

The following is a direct quote from the publicity material produced by the software company:

Moviestorm is a software application that enables you to make animated videos on your computer. It's a full suite of movie-making tools with which you can simply create and light your own sets, design and direct your own actors, then shoot, edit and publish your own movies.

Key features include:

- Intuitive click and explore game-style interface
- Pre-made customizable sets, characters and movies
- Thousands of characters, costumes, sets, props and animations, suitable for most film projects
- Flexible personalization options for props, characters and much more
- Import your own assets, including music, models and textures
- A suite of tools that encourages teamwork and fun
- No animation or artist skills required to be creative
- Upload direct to YouTube, or your preferred social network
- A highly supportive community of amateur and professional movie-makers at www.moviestorm.co.uk

Materials:

- A PC or Mac that's capable of playing recent games such as *World of Warcraft*
- Speakers or headphones, to listen to your audio
- A microphone, if you want your actors to talk

Moviestorm can be tried for free before deciding upon a range of rental or purchase options. For the latest information on pricing, go to www.moviestorm.co.uk.

MAKING A MOVIE WITH MOVIESTORM

set
props exterior
personalise
textures lighting
colour
interior customise

characters
*age*ethnicity
morph accessorise
hairstyles
makeup
decals costumes

direct
*dialogue*emotions
special effects
control
interactions
gestures
objects

cameras
pan
frame one-shot
depth of field free
zoom multiple
cut
target

edit
titles *filters*
credits
music
shake
import
sound effects

publish 3D
resolution
social network
record
upload share

Moviestorm

Colour versions of these images
can be found on the companion website

PART FOUR: SCHEMES OF WORK

4.1 TELL ME A STORY

Project brief:
Students storyboarded and filmed short stories inspired by traditional fairy tales or folk tales from a different culture. They learned how to present a narrative using 2D cut-out animation techniques.

The objectives were:

- to create an animation using a pre-existing story as the stimulus

- to begin to understand the dynamic relationship between the written word and animation

- to work collaboratively in groups and to engage the entire class

- to develop ideas and storyboards based on tales from different cultures

- to develop characterization, a script and storyboard for an animation

- to create artwork such as sets and props

- to capture the animation using stop-motion software and use software to edit

- to use ICT and software effectively and creatively

Stage 1: Storyboarding
In groups of four to five pupils, students selected stories from different cultures. Each group adapted their story and transformed it into a storyboard for a 20-second animation.

Hints and tips:

We asked the students to write the story using the standard narrative convention of third person, past tense. This included a narrator's voice and/or dialogue by the main characters. Students used a maximum of 60 words, and about 6 sentences. Referring back to the original text, they maintained the overall structure of the original storyline, that is, they established the main characters and the scenario, quest or dilemma facing the characters and how it is resolved or completed.

They storyboarded the tale in six shots, one per sentence in the script.

They added a description of the action taking place under each shot and listed sound effects.

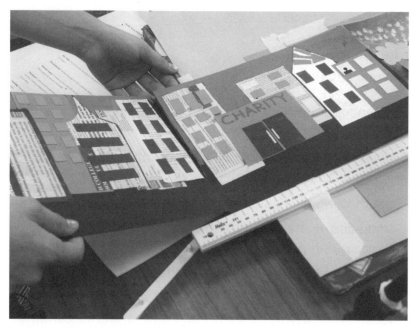

Background art work

Stage 2: Production

We allocated two lessons to storyboarding, and three lessons to model making and set building. The production stage needed three full school days to shoot the animations, compose the music, record sound effects and narration and edit.

Stage 3: Assessment
Expectations

At the end of this project most pupils explored ideas and made moving images in response to an existing story and identified the key components of story; character, narrative and meaning. They researched fairy tales and the history of animated film. They were able to organize and use visual and other information in their work and manipulate media to convey their ideas. They analysed and commented on their own and others' images and related this to what was intended. They adapted their work to refine their own ideas and intentions.

The more advanced students were able to exploit the characteristics of the media, analyse and comment on the context of their own and others' work and explain how their own ideas have influenced their practice.

Prior learning
It is helpful if students have:

- developed the habit of reading and comprehending what they have read
- developed the habit of collecting visual and other sources of information to support their work
- used collage, model-making and mark-making techniques
- used digital images and the internet as an integral part of their art and design work
- compared the moving image with other forms of visual imagery and considered their varying impacts
- looked critically at their own and others' work in order to generate ideas for adapting and developing their work

Language for learning
Through the activities in this unit pupils should be able to understand and use vocabulary relating to:

- written narratives and scripting
- the moving image, for example, composition, close-up, focus, viewpoint, viewer, kinetic, the representation of time, sound and sense of space, narrative, overlay, harmony, movement, rhythm
- methods and processes, for example, collage, montage, storyboard, cartoon, illustration
- equipment, for example, ICT, digital camera, photographic camera, film camera, video camera, optical toys, projectors, image manipulation

Future learning

Individual students should ideally be given opportunities to develop their technical control of materials and processes and develop ideas for individual work for GCSE Art examination. Skills learned could also transfer to 'A' level Art, Photography and Media Studies.

Adapting the project

Students could generate their own stories but in using established fairy tales they engage with a useful template for narrative structure. It is useful to provide students with a selection of lesser-known fairy tales so as to avoid plagiarism of well-known films.

Assessment

Each student needs to ensure that they keep a record of their own individual contribution to enable consistent moderation.

Individual contributions could include:

- ideas and storyboards
- analysis of existing animations
- artwork, such as sets and characters
- the finished media artefacts

Resources:

Video clip: SOW 1: Tell me a Story ⌐🖱
Animation Styles: **Cut-Out Animation:** p. 85 of this book.

Animations by: Oskar Fischinger, Jan Svankmajer, Caroline Leaf, Petra Freeman, Ruth Lingford, Jonathan Hodgson, Lotte Reiniger, Aardman and Studio Ghibli. (See **A Brief History** p. 9 and **Recommended Animators** p. 150.)

Animated Films that use fairy tales and pre-existing stories as a basis:

- *Snow White and the Seven Dwarfs*
- *Pinocchio*
- *Beauty and the Beast*
- *Cinderella*
- *Peter and the Wolf*
- *Watership Down*
- *Azur and Asmar*
- *The Story*teller television series

The fairytales used came from the following sources:

The Tortoise and the Geese and other Fables of Bidpai, retold by Maude Barrows Dutton (Boston: Houghton Mifflin Company, 1908), pp. 22–23

Tikki Tikki Tembo, retold by Arlene Mosel, illustrated by Blair Lent (New York: Holt, Rinehart, and Winston, 1968)

Folklore of the Santal Parganas, translated by Cecil Henry Bompas of the Indian Civil Service (London: David Nutt, 1909) no. 146, pp. 372–373

Joseph Jacobs, *More English Fairy Tales* (New York and London: G. P. Putnam's Sons, n.d.), pp. 107–109. This collection was first published in 1894

The Jataka; or, Stories of the Buddha's Former Births, edited by E. B. Cowell (Cambridge University Press, 1895), book 1, no. 44

The Bremen Town Musicians by Jacob and Wilhelm Grimm:
http://www.bremen-tourismus.de/english/k1-rubrik_unter.cfm?Index=1504&m=1.&RubrikID=1515&RubrikID2=&lang=eng

Storyboarding

4.2 TV ADVERTS

Project brief:

The task was to create a 20-second TV advertisement to support the Arms Control Campaign. In this activity, pupils explored the use of animation in television advertising of products and ideas. They studied a number of animated commercials. They learned how to represent ideas and values using the moving image.

This project can become part of GCSE Art and Design or Photography coursework. It could also be adapted for Year 9 groups (age 13) and become a cross-curricular project involving Music and Media Studies. This scheme of work can be linked to the citizenship curriculum, where pupils are encouraged to discuss moral and social issues, by analysing information and its sources, including ICT-based sources.

Students devised a 30-second TV advert on a theme of Human Rights. They worked in groups of three or four producing an advertisement supporting a 'Human Rights' campaign. Each group selected one or more of the issues listed below and storyboarded a sequence drawing public attention to it.

1. Control Arms (joint campaign with Oxfam).
2. Stop Violence against women.
3. End the trade in conflict diamonds.
4. Stop torture in the war on terror.
5. Refugees and asylum seekers.
6. Defend the defenders, support for human rights campaigners in danger.

They used one or more of the following techniques; drawn animation over photographed backgrounds and/or 2D cut-out animation (with art work from newspapers, magazines or photographic sources). They were given time to add their own composed music.

The objectives were:

• to work collaboratively in groups working to an industry-style brief

- to develop characterization, a script and storyboard for an animation
- to make a set and props
- to capture the animation using stop-motion techniques and use software to edit
- to record all stages of the project for GCSE work journals
- to create effective artwork
- to use ICT and software effectively

This scheme of work took four full school days to complete, when assigned to a group of 14-year-old students. It involved one day of storyboarding and preparing art work, two days of production, and one day of post-production. This was supported by a prior cineliteracy day to introduce animation history and literacy.

Stage 1: Storyboarding and pre-production

Students prepared storyboards, selecting a range of four to five different types of shot including close-up, medium shots and wide/ establishing shots.

They identified all backgrounds, characters and props required and prepared these.

Stage 2: Production

Working in small teams, students shot the scenes in the storyboards. They added additional cutaways or alternative takes as required. They assembled and reviewed the scenes as a rough cut. They checked that the narration and/or dialogue fitted and adapted it as needed.

Stage 3: Post-Production

Students recorded and captured all required dialogue, narration and sound effects. They composed background and titles music using the software package Acid. They edited the images and sounds together using Premiere Pro.

They discussed and evaluated the end results with the rest of the class.

Editing using Premiere Pro

Stage 4: Assessment

At the end of this project most pupils had:

- explored ideas and values and ways to express them via the language of the moving image
- researched contemporary advertising and the history of animated film
- organized and used visual and other information in their work
- analysed and commented on their own and others' images and related this to what was intended
- adapted their work to refine their own ideas and intentions

The more advanced students exploited the characteristics of the media and made choices about using them, analysed and commented on the context of their own and others' work and explained how their own ideas had influenced their practice.

Prior learning

It is helpful if students have:

- developed the habit of collecting visual and other sources of information to support their work

- used collage, model-making and mark-making techniques
- used digital images and the internet as an integral part of their art and design work
- compared the moving image with other forms of visual imagery and considered their varying impacts
- developed the habit of reflecting on their own and others' work in order to generate ideas for adapting and developing their work

Language for learning

Through the activities in this unit pupils should be able to understand and use vocabulary relating to:

- the moving image, for example, composition, close-up, focus, viewpoint, viewer, kinetic, the representation of time, sound and sense of space, narrative, overlay, harmony, movement, rhythm
- methods and processes, for example, collage, montage, storyboard, cartoon, illustration
- equipment, for example, ICT, digital camera, photographic camera, film camera, video camera, optical toys, projectors, image manipulation

Future learning

Individual students should ideally be given opportunities to develop their technical control of materials and processes and develop ideas for individual work for GCSE Art examinations. Skills learned could also transfer to 'A' level Art, Photography and Media Studies.

Assessment

Each student needs to ensure that they keep a record of their own individual contribution to enable consistent moderation.

Individual contributions could include

- ideas and storyboards
- analysis of existing animations
- artwork, such as sets and characters
- the finished media artefacts

Resources:

Video clip: SOW 2: TV Adverts 🖱

Worksheet: Cut-Out Figures: p. 85 of this book.

Citizenship issues: http://www.controlarms.org

TV advertisements using animation:

http://www.videosift.com/video/Len-Lye-A-Colour-Box-Free-Radicals

Hands Guinness Ad:
http://www.youtube.com/watch?v=IQDjynOzgCk

TV commercial history:

http://www.aardman.com/commercials/

http://en.wikipedia.org/wiki/History_of_animation

http://www.vod.com/video/36131/History-Of-Advertising-Animation-1940-1950/

http://www.aaacaricatures.com/hannabarberacartoons.html

4.3 MUSIC VIDEOS

This scheme of work took five full school days to complete, when assigned to a group of 15- to 16-year-old students. We began with a cineliteracy day to introduce animated music video history, languages and genres. This was followed by one day of storyboarding and set building, two days of production, and one day of post-production and evaluation.

In line with national averages, of the 17 students involved 4 have some kind of learning difficulty. The animation project enabled these students to achieve in a way that I had not witnessed before. They became confident and articulate, in part due to working within a safe environment for a concentrated amount of time, but also due to the high expectations placed upon them and their loyalty to the group.

(Sally Hurst Head of Art and Design)

Music video history

Students were introduced to the history of music videos and shown examples, such as *Madness, Aha, Peter Gabriel, Tom Tom Club, Gorillaz* and *Nizlopi*. A critical discussion took place, exploring the intended audiences and markets for videos by *Gorillaz*.

- Why are *Gorillaz* famous while others are less well-known?
- Why is animation used?
- What techniques of animation were used?
- Which do you prefer and why?
- Which would you be more prepared to spend money on?
- Which cost more to make?
- Write a list of other animated music videos you have seen. Which do you like and why?

Project brief

In small groups, students designed a virtual band, and considered how it will be marketed. They began by planning a 1-minute music video to promote the band. They selected an animation style from the following options: plasticine model animation, drawn animation, cut-out animation, live action and animation combined using blue screen.

Stage 1: Storyboarding and pre-production

Students prepared a storyboard for their 1-minute video. They considered how the action will relate to the lyrics and musical style of the song.

They considered the following questions:

Production:

- How will your selected style influence the visual content, storyline and music?
- How will you organize yourselves into a production team and delegate tasks?

Language:

- What are the most effective ways of getting your message across?
- Will you use well-known conventions or genres or subvert them in some way?

Representation:

- What ideas or values are you trying to convey?
- How do you want to represent the world?
- Are you using stereotypes and, if so, what are the consequences of doing so?

Audience:

- Who are you communicating to, and why?
- What assumptions are you making about your audience?
- How are you going to persuade them to watch the video and listen to, or buy the music?

Stage 2: Production

- The students adopted a wide range of animation styles. One team used bluescreen techniques to integrate their pixilated characters into a cut-out and live action world. We used a portable bluescreen system, available from Backdropsource for around £220. Details here:

- http://www.backdropsource.co.uk/Productinfo. asp?id=727&pname=3mx-6.3m-chroma-key-blue-muslin-backdrop-with-a-stand

- Other teams used a variety of cut-out and drawn animation techniques.

Stage 3: Post-Production

For the examples shown on the companion website (SOW 3: Music Videos) a professional composer helped the students write their songs and edit them to the animations. The software used was Acid Pro 6, published by Sony, used alongside a collection of DVD-based sound samples. Acid Pro retails for around £125 for an educational licence, and is targeted at both professionals and serious amateurs. (The sound sample libraries must be purchased separately.) A free alternative sound editing package, for schools on a tight budget, is Audacity. See p. 132 for further details.

Lyrics and live instruments were recorded directly onto the laptop hard drives, using Acid Pro, and an external microphone.

The finished songs were exported as wav format files into Adobe Premiere Pro or Pinnacle Studio, where the animations were edited to the songs. The students completed their own editing, with support from a professional animator. The more able students were able to quickly learn the basics of editing themselves, without extensive guidance.

Stage 4: Assessment

For assessment guidance, see the previous scheme of work.
In addition to this, we asked the students to evaluate their own work using this format:

Part One: The process

Explain briefly the animation you made and how you made it.

Which kind of music did your group create/choose to animate and why?

What roles did the various people in the group take? Describe in detail your role in the various activities.

What tasks had to be done in the research and planning phase? How were these handled and what could have been done to improve them?

How did the group come to decisions about approaches to the tasks to be completed?

What factors were involved in the choices you made in constructing the artwork for the animation?

What tasks had to be done in shooting and editing the animation? How were these handled and what could have been done to improve them?

Part Two: The product

Analyse the images and editing in your finished animation, paying close attention to artwork, narrative and mise-en-scene and the ways in which you have constructed the animation to fit the music in terms of both style and construction.

How well do you feel the product fulfils the initial brief?

What did the audience think of your animation?

What changes would you have made in light of your own analysis and feedback from others?

Resources:

Video clips: SOW3: Music Videos:

Music video by Nizlopi using drawn animation:
http://www.youtube.com/nizlopi#p/search/0/16OqP6F0Jqo

Madness–Baggy Trousers:
   http://www.youtube.com/watch?v=XJOLwy7un3U

Aha–Take on Me: http://www.youtube.com/watch?v=djV11Xbc914

Peter Gabriel–Sledgehammer:
   http://www.youtube.com/watch?v=hqyc37aOqT0

Videos by Gorillaz: http://www.gorillaz.com/flash.html

Wikipedia: A History of music videos:
   http://en.wikipedia.org/wiki/Music_video

Publication: Teaching Music Video BFI 2004, Editor Vivienne Clark

PART FIVE: RESOURCES

5.1 ANIMATION EQUIPMENT

Setting up an animation rostrum does not have to be expensive. However, the market now offers a huge range of cheap video cameras and recording formats, making it difficult to choose the best model for classroom work. Here are a few tips regarding the pros and cons of the different types. You need to consider the entire production route before making a decision.

MiniDV-based SD or HDV camcorders
These record to cheap mini DV format tapes in standard or high definition, in 4:3 format or 16:9 widescreen. They support Firewire, making them easy to connect to a laptop for stop-frame animation. (Some models also support USB 2.) They work with most stop-motion software. Standard definition files can be captured and edited in any editing software. (See 5.3 **Animation Software** for choices.)

We strongly recommend this format for schools on a tight budget.

However, these camcorders are getting harder to find, as manufacturers are now heavily promoting the new high-definition formats such as AVCHD (see below).

DVD-R and HDD camcorders
These record video in the DVD format directly to small DVD disks or hard drives. This format is not suitable for editing real-time video using software such as Premiere. These cameras are not normally compatible with stop-motion software. **Not recommended.**

AVCHD camcorders
These record full high-definition video in a range of highly compressed formats. Most of these new generation cameras record straight to memory cards.

For smooth real-time editing you will need a fast desktop or laptop computer with Core 2 Duo or Quad processors or better. To guarantee real-time playback on a wider range of Apple and PC computers we recommend capturing your video using a Matrox MX02 Mini. This captures your Hi-definition video to an edit-friendly file format in real time. It has HDMI, component, SVideo and composite in and out and works at up to 1920 x 1080 resolution. It therefore solves the problem that many of the newer AVCHD cameras do not support Firewire. Instead, you can capture live action video or stop-motion frames using either an HDMI or component cable.

Stop-motion capture is achieved using the bundled software. However, bear in mind that your animation will be captured as a series of still images, which must be rendered as an animation in a software packages such as Premiere Pro. As such, this production route is not particularly user-friendly.

The MX02 mini currently costs around £320 plus VAT and comes in two versions. The Express card version connects to laptops, and the PCIe card version connects to desktop computers.

Another way to capture HD animation from an AVCHD camcorder to a desktop PC is to buy a Black Magic Intensity Pro HDMI capture card (approx. £150 incl VAT) and software such as Stop Motionmaker HDMI (approx. £35) or Stop Motion Pro Action! HD (around £190 for a school licence—one workstation). Bear in mind, you cannot use the capture card with a laptop.

AVCHD-based video and animation can be edited using Pinnacle Studio 14 (around £50), Premiere Pro CS5 (around £320 education price), Premiere Elements (around £70) or Edius Neo 2 (about £185). Further information on editing software for PCs and Macs can be found on p. 136.

Choose the AVCHD format if you are able to invest in fast computers and high end animation and editing solutions.

SETTING UP AN ANIMATION ROSTRUM

You will need the following:

A digital camcorder

These cost from £125 to £3000 depending on quality. (See 5.1 for further details.) We recommend a mini DV camcorder with DVin/out via firewire. Choose a 3CCD model for superior image quality, if budget allows.

A robust tripod

Choose a tripod which is stable. Ideally pick one with a fluid head, as this will be useful for live action film making as well. They cost from £30 to £200 for basic models.

Headphones

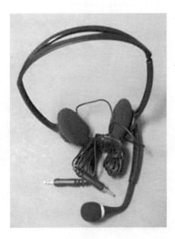

It is best to choose a set of closed ear-style headphones, which help to exclude ambient sound, letting you focus on the actual recorded signal (price approx. £30–£100). The headset shown includes a microphone, which is handy for basic soundtrack recording. However, for more advanced sound work we strongly recommend using a separate microphone. (See 5.2 for details.)

A desktop computer or laptop

Laptops are preferable to desktop computers for two reasons. First, as they are portable they can be easily moved to a temporary rostrum setting. Secondly, they can be used independently of a school network, which avoids potential problems relating to data transfer speeds and software networking.

The example shows a close-up of the sockets you are likely to need: Left to right: microphone, headphone, 4 pin firewire port and two USB sockets.

A 5-metre firewire cable

You will need a 5-metre firewire cable, so that the camera can be set up a safe distance from the table or drawing board containing the animation set. The length also allows the cable to be taped out of the way of moving animators.

There are two standards: a 4 pin and a 6 pin. PC laptops and camcorders favour the 4 pin socket. Apple computers and laptops use the 6 pin version. Sometimes, you will need to buy 4 pin to 6 pin cables.

Note that some camcorders do not support firewire (see 5.1 for alternative cable requirements).

A studio light

A colour version of this image
can be found on the companion website

Ideally, each rostrum should be lit by a studio quality light
on a sturdy stand. The one shown burns cool, so is safe for
the classroom. You can buy a three or one bulb version from
Backdropsource for around £40–£70.

http://www.backdropsource.co.uk/Productinfo.
asp?id=1143&pname=90-watt-ultra-cool-light-with-stand

Setting up a 3D table top rostrum

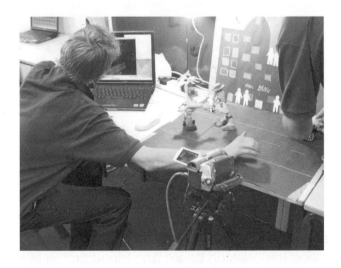

For 3D work, such as plasticine animation, you will need to position the tripod to point across to the set. Place the laptop next to the animation set, leaving room for the animators to work either side of the set. Make sure all cables are taped down.

Setting up a 2D rostrum

For 2D work, such as cut-out animation, ensure the tripod is fully extended, with the camera pointing down on the art work. Tape down the legs of the tripod to help avoid accidental movement. The camera must be at least 1 metre from the art work to ensure sharp focus. (Check this by zooming right in on the art work.) Use a drawing board, and tilt it up slightly to prevent parallax problems. Sometimes it is easier to place the drawing board and tripod on the floor.

Technical and safety tips

Use of space:
Try to arrange the rostrums in the room to allow plenty of space for the students to work, without crowding each other. Place the set so two students can work either side, moving one or more characters each. Place the laptop so a third student can capture frames beside the animators. Make sure the laptop is positioned so the animators can see the composition on the screen, and reference it when adjusting model positions.

Lighting:
If you do not have access to studio lights, choose a place where the light will remain constant throughout the session. Intermittent sunlight falling on the art work will ruin a sequence. If you do have lights, use one per rostrum, set to one side, away from traffic and above students' heads. Warn the students that the lights can get very hot, and should never be touched or moved without teacher assistance. Energy-saving lights burn cooler, and are safer for classroom work. (See example above.)

Tripods and camerawork:
Tripods should only be adjusted while setting up a shot, before animation begins. Never force the tripod, always unlock it before panning or tilting and hold the pan bar to adjust. After this, the tripod and camera should not be touched. Students will always want to look in the viewfinder, and play with the camera controls while animating. This must be avoided. Remind them that they can check the composition on the laptop. Compositions should not be changed until the shot is complete. Zooming or panning does not work well for stop-frame animation (without special professional tools).

Cables:
It is vital to tape down all cables with gaffer tape to avoid tripping over them. Pay particular attention to the firewire cable. Tape it down close to the socket connections at the camera and the laptop, with some slack at the camera end so it can be adjusted between shots.

5.2 RECORDING AND EDITING SOUND

Sound is as important as the image in creating a successful animation. It should never be considered an afterthought. When budgeting for a moving image facility in your school, consider spending as much on a good microphone system as you would a video camera.

Most professional sound recordists use a shotgun or short shotgun microphone for recording dialogue and interviews. Its sensitivity is very directional, so you must point it precisely at the subject or desired sound source. Unwanted background sounds are minimized.

A wind shield is essential for outdoor work to eliminate wind noise, and a cradle to hold the microphone will minimize handling noise. A fish pole or boom is very useful for drama work, as it enables the recordist to position the mic above the actors' heads. Always place the mic as close as you can without intruding on the shot. The ideal placement for recording dialogue is about 30 cm from the speaker's lips.

A good set of headphones is essential. Choose a closed set, so you just hear the sound being recorded. Most importantly, listen carefully for problems such as distortion and unwanted background sound.

Most domestic camcorders provide a socket for connecting an external mic. It is never a good idea to rely on the internal camcorder mic. First, the recording quality is usually inferior. Secondly, you cannot place the mic where you want it to record the sound source. Finally, it will record all the camera handling noise, tape transport, zoom servo etc.

Cheaper cameras only provide a mini jack socket, designed to take low-cost microphones with unbalanced leads. Unbalanced leads have a single signal carrying cable, and are prone to radio interference, which can ruin a recording. The longer the cable, the worse the problem gets.

Better microphones use balanced cables with XLR plugs and sockets, designed to eliminate interference. To use a balanced microphone with a cheap DV camcorder, you need a Beachtek audio adaptor (£200). This connects to the bottom of the camera, and provides two XLR sockets for your microphone system.

For recording direct to a laptop, running software such as Audacity, a stereo microphone with a stereo mini jack plug is ideal. (Interference is unlikely, because of the short cable length.) Good headphones are still important!

EQUIPMENT OPTIONS

Balanced cable options for live action video and animation
Sennheiser ME66/K6 short shotgun mic system: around £400

Rycote Windshield 4 kit: around £325

XLR cable 5 metre around £25

fish pole: around £48 headphones: £25–£50

Cheaper mic options:
Clockaudio C850E short shotgun mic with windshield: around £200

or 3208850 shotgun mic: around £55

Stereo minijack-based options suitable for recording direct to a laptop:
Audio Technica Pro 24 Stereo Condenser mic: around £70

Beyer 210/7 mic stand with boom: around £25

Please check the internet for latest models and prices.

Equipment suppliers:
http://www.canford.co.uk/

PC-BASED AUDIO EDITING WITH AUDACITY

Audacity is free, open source software for the multi-track recording and editing of sounds. It is simple and extremely effective to use allowing both the importing and exporting of sound files in WAV and MP3 formats. It enables the recording of sound directly on to the hard disc of a PC either by microphone or direct feed. This is achieved through the microphone mini jack port.

Audacity can be downloaded at:

http://audacity.sourceforge.net/download/windows?lang=en

You will need a PC running Windows XP, Vista or 7 (including Windows Movie Maker), a microphone or a means of transferring sound from an original source (e.g. a direct feed from MIDI sequencer with appropriate cabling).

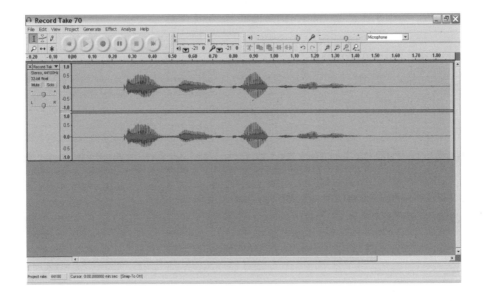

Features include:

- level and L/R positioning controls for each track
- I/O level and L/R positioning controls
- simple editing features: cut, copy, paste, trim etc.

- viewing options
- project organizing functions: import MIDI, new tracks, track alignment etc.
- sound generator: white noise, tone, silence, click track etc.
- effects: fade in, fade out, reverse, boost bass etc.
- analysis tool: beat finder, silence finder etc.

Audacity is an easy tool to use to record sound effects, voices or music for animation.

Step by step guide:

- Select file new.
- Make sure the microphone is plugged in, headphones ready.
- To record a new track, click the red record button and the recording
- starts immediately.
- Record, counting to 20, moving closer and further away from the microphone.
- See the difference in the waveforms and hear the difference in quality.
- Press playback to hear the recording.
- Highlight your sound file with the selection tool and try some effects,
- e.g. reverse or tempo.
- Read the help files to see what else you can do.
- For video editing you **must** export your sound file as wav files!

Hints and tips:

Try not to record voices or sound for the entire animation sequence in a single take. Record one item at a time. It might help to have a 'rough edit' to look at so you can prepare a wish list of sound effects, music or narration.

Keep all your files in one folder! Keep it tidy and organized.

Using a click track

Assuming that you already have some ideas for the music, and in particular its tempo, you need to create a click track.

Once the tempo of the music has been decided, Audacity can be used to generate the click track. Click Generate>Click track in the drop-down menu. The options will be given for the tempo, beats per measure and number of measures. Compound click tracks can be created by inserting additional tracks, for each of which you will generate a new click to match each tempo change. These can then be copied and pasted into the main click track.

Most commercially produced music, including film music, uses a click track. The only exceptions to this tend to be on jazz and classical music recordings. The system is very simple and a way of coordinating, by means of a regular metronomic pulse, the performance of the musicians involved. The click is fed to the performers via headphones, and in the bigger films, it is often the case that there may be as many as 100 sets of headphones in use at one time.

Once the click track has been prepared it can be saved as either a WAV or MP3 file for insertion into Windows Movie Maker.

The click track coordinates with the film and runs at the tempo of the music. There will be a preparatory set of bars where only the click is heard and then the film itself will kick in. Generally, music that is at a different tempo from the preceding section will be recorded separately, although it is sometimes the case that a compound click track is prepared in which the tempi may change. This was very much the case in the film *Who Framed Roger Rabbit* where the composer, Alan Silvestri, prepared a score much in the style of the old animation cartoons of Tom and Jerry, with many frequent tempo changes.

For recording compound click tracks with changes of tempi, first add more tracks. Click Project>New audio track and for each track generate a new click corresponding to each change of tempo. Cut and paste these into the master click track. Ensure that you have included some free beats before the point where the music starts by way of a countdown–for example, two measures of four beats.

After all the adjustments have been made to the master track, delete the others.

Save the master click track as a WAV or MP3 file for importing into Windows Movie Maker or another editing package.

Sound editing

5.3 STOP-MOTION ANIMATION SOFTWARE

DRAGON STOP MOTION

There are many software packages available for both the PC and the Mac, at a wide range of price points. The product which gets our strongest recommendation is Dragon Stop Motion. It is a powerful, professional quality tool, with many advanced features. Some of these may be beyond the needs of the typical classroom project. However, its ease of use, quality and versatility makes it well worth the price. (Currently around £250 for two school licences.)

With Dragon Stop Motion you can connect SD or HD video camcorders via firewire to a desktop or laptop computer, a PC or a Mac. Alternatively, you can use a wide range of Digital SLRs and other digital still cameras, connected via USB. We particularly like the onion skin facility, which helps students to judge exactly how far to move characters between frames.

The software works by capturing preview quality frames for instant playback, alongside high-quality frames at SD, HD or feature film resolution, depending on the image source used and setting selected. The latter can then be rendered as mov video files and imported to your preferred editing software for post-production.

To quote the website: 'A stop motion software tool for creating stop-frame animation, 3D stereoscopic animation, time-lapse, digital effects, and claymation. It is compatible with Mac OS X and Windows XP/Vista/Windows 7 PC computers and can be used with a digital still camera, video camera or webcam. Designed to meet the needs of working professionals, yet intuitive enough for beginners. It is used widely for feature film, commercial, broadcast television and independent film.'

Download a trial version and get further details here:

http://www.dragonstopmotion.com/

USING DRAGON STOP MOTION IN THE CLASSROOM

The following advice makes the assumption that you are already familiar with using Dragon Stop Motion. (If not, then these tutorial videos provide an excellent overview: http://www.dragonstopmotion. com/tutorials.php)

We recommend using the following production settings when working with students. This approach will provide you with rendered files containing two exposures per animation movement with a high picture quality. You will actually only capture one exposure per image movement, for the fastest possible workflow.

When using a widescreen standard definition camcorder:
In the Camera Settings window, use these settings: Image Size: 100%. Compression: Highest Quality. Aspect Ratio: Wide. Noise Reduction: On. Resolution: Custom: 1024 x 576

In the Animate window, set playback to 12.5 fps. This will simulate playback at 25 fps, as if you are shooting two exposures per image movement.

Capture exposures should be left in the default Single Frame mode.

When you render the take as a Quicktime movie for import into an editing program, use these settings:

Make a compressed, self-contained movie at high resolution, with pixel dimensions of 1024 x 576. Make sure the frame rate is set to 12.5 fps. In this way, the movie will render with two exposures of each image capture and playback on the timeline at the same frame rate as the preview did.

Use the DV Pal compressor at the highest setting, set to 16.9 aspect ratio, with the frame rate set to 12.5 fps.

The end result will be suitable for DVD production or publishing on the internet after further compression.

When using an HDV camcorder or still camera:
In the Camera Settings window, use these settings: Image Size: 100%. Compression: Highest Quality. Aspect Ratio: Wide. Noise Reduction: On. Resolution: Custom: 1920 x 1080.

Make a compressed, self-contained movie at high resolution, with pixel dimensions of 1920 x 1080. Make sure the frame rate is set to 12.5 fps.

Use MPEG 4 compression at the best setting.

If you want the best quality possible, use the animation setting when selecting a codec. The files will be much bigger as no extra compression is used. However, you will be hard-pressed to notice any improvement in image quality if you are using a video camera as your image source.

Other hints and tips:
If using a video or still camera, place the aperture, gain, shutter speed and focus in manual mode, so none of these settings change between exposures. (Many cheaper camcorders do not give you control over all these settings, so you may still see fluctuations in exposure and focus when you play back your animation.)

Make sure your subject is sharp and correctly exposed before you begin shooting.

If you work in HDV, the process of capturing both the video assist frame and a high definition tiff or jpeg still frame can take up to 6 seconds (as compared to 2 seconds in standard definition). You will hear a shutter sound effect as soon as the video assist frame is captured, followed by a beep after the still frame has been captured. Animators must wait for the beep before moving their models again, otherwise hands will be recorded on the high-quality still frames!

OTHER PC-BASED SOLUTIONS

Stop Motion Pro is a software tool for making stop motion and other animated films. It requires a video camera, webcam or digital still camera and be compatible with Win XP or Vista. See: *www. stopmotionpro.com*

AnimatorDV is a PC-based software for creating stop-motion and time-lapse animation. Can be also used on a film set as a previsualization tool.

See: http://animatordv.com/

Monkeyjam and a simple webcam is a £5.00 animation solution!

See: http://www.giantscreamingrobotmonkeys.com/monkeyjam/index.html

Toon Boom Studio
Toon Boom Studio is a vector-based drawn animation tool, discussed on p. 98. See: http://www.toonboom.com

Serif DrawPlus
DrawPlus is Serif's award winning vector-based drawing package, ideal for use in schools. See: http://www.serif.com/drawplus/

DigiCel Flip Book
A professional drawn animation package. See: http://www.digicelinc.com

Moovl
Moovl makes drawings spring into life. Moovl imbues freehand drawings with bouncy physics and animated behaviours, and can be used on an interactive whiteboard or tablet PC.

See: http://www.moovl.co.uk/

Scratch
Scratch is a programming language that makes it easy to create interactive stories, animations, games, music and art–and share your creations on the web.

See: http://info.scratch.mit.edu/About_Scratch

OTHER MAC-BASED SOLUTIONS

iStopMotion
Easy to use Stop-Motion animation software for Mac OS X. Allows you to use your computer and DV camcorder or USB webcams to capture single frames for stop motion

See: http://www.boinx.com/istopmotion/overview/

FrameThief
FrameThief is a software package for creating animation on the Macintosh platform

See: http://www.framethief.com

BTV Pro supports movie playback and editing, stop-motion animation, time-lapse capture, motion detection, DV stream input/ output and frame averaging.

See: http://www.bensoftware.com

I Can Animate has established itself as a popular Stop-Motion Animation tool for Mac OS X.

See: http://www.kudlian.net/products/icananimate/

With **Frames** (PC Windows or Mac) students can create stop-motion animated stories using pictures of clay characters they make, stop-motion pictures from a DV or USB camera, pictures they have taken with a digital camera or pictures they have drawn or painted in.

StopMotioner is a full featured stop-motion creation tool (aka Clay Animation). It contains all the necessary tools to capture, edit and share your stop-motion movies. No need to import your clips to another program for editing; it contains all the tools you need and more while retaining the original quality. Edit in StopMotioner as you capture—adding titles, transitions and audio.

See: http://www.miensoftware.com/stopmotioner.html

StopMojo is cross-platform stop-motion animation suite designed to aid in the creation of stop-motion animations. Currently it includes a capture program supporting capture of image files from various video capture devices, overlay of previous frames (onion skinning) and export to AVI and QUICKTIME video formats.

See: http://www.mondobeyondo.com/projects/stopmojo/

5.4 VIDEO AND ANIMATION EDITING

EDITING SOFTWARE: PC SOLUTIONS

Pinnacle Studio

Pinnacle Studio represents excellent value for money as a video editing solutions for schools. It provides support for the entire production workflow, from capture to editing and export to a wide range of platforms and media. It supports SD, HDV and AVCHD video formats. It includes stop-motion capture, eliminating the need for separate software. It is also available in a Mac version. See: http://www.pinnaclesys.com/PublicSite/uk/Products/ Consumer+Products/Home+Video/Studio+Family/

Windows Movie Maker

Movie Maker is a free (with Windows PCs) entry-level solution, suitable for schools projects. See. p. 144 for a step by step guide. To download the latest version look here: http://download.live.com/ moviemaker

For an XP compatible version look here:

http://www.microsoft.com/windowsxp/downloads/updates/ moviemaker2.mspx

Adobe Premiere Elements / Adobe Premiere Pro

Premiere Elements is an entry-level version of Adobe's professional video-editing program, Premiere Pro. It includes stop-motion capture, eliminating the need for separate software.

Premiere Pro is an ideal choice for KS4 and A Level students considering a career in the creative industries. It is a fully featured platform allowing complex industry standard editing tasks. However, it does not include stop-motion capture.

See: http://www.adobe.com/uk/products/premiere/

EDITING SOFTWARE: MAC SOLUTIONS

iMovie
iMovie is simple and fast to learn. In just a few steps, you can add movies to your website, publish them on YouTube, and create versions for iPod, iPhone and Apple TV.

See: http://www.apple.com/ilife/imovie/

Final Cut Pro
A professional editing platform supporting live action. Animators will also need a stop-motion capture tool such as Dragon Stop Motion.

See: http://www.apple.com/finalcutstudio/finalcutpro/

EDITING WITH WINDOWS MOVIE MAKER

Windows Movie Maker is included free with all Windows operating systems. It provides all the tools needed to edit a simple animation with one soundtrack (music, narration or sound effects), titles, credits and transitions.

Importing video clips:
Open Window Movie Maker, click on the File menu and start a new project. Import your video files into Collections. (Warning: long files can take several minutes to import.)

Select 'Show Timeline' by clicking on the film icon above the timeline. Drag your video files in the required order onto the timeline. You can trim unwanted material from the start and end of clips by hovering your mouse pointer over the left or right hand edge of the clip. It will turn into a red double-headed arrow. Hold down the left mouse to drag the clip shorter. Place the timeline cursor over the area you wish to edit. Use the plus icon to zoom in to the timeline for greater accuracy. You can preview your edit in the video preview window.

Adding sound:
Import your sound files (in the wav format) and drag them underneath the animation clips into the Audio/Music line. Trim if necessary. Right click on the sound file to reveal additional options such as Fade In, Fade Out and Volume. Clicking on Volume allows you to adjust the sound level of the clip.

Narrating a voice over or sound effects:
Select Narrate Timeline from the Tools menu. Plug in your mic and test the mic volume using the pop up VU meter. Adjust the input level to avoid distortion. Place the timeline cursor at the point in the edit where you want your narration to begin. (Note: The Start Narration button will ghost out if you place the cursor over an existing sound clip. If placed at the start of the timeline, it will overwrite an existing clip.) Name the file you have created. It will be placed on the timeline for you. Click Done. Adjust the volume level on the timeline if needed.

Titles and credits:

To add a title or credits click on Titles or Credits in the Tools menu and follow the instructions in the pop-up wizard. Drag the title clip to the Title Overlay line if you wish to superimpose it over your live video.

Video transitions:

Open the Video Transitions menu from the Tools menu. Select the transition you want and drag it between two video clips on the timeline. It will appear in the Transition line on the timeline.

Video effects:

Open the Video Effects menu and drag your effect onto the desired video clip. Fade In, From Black and Fade Out, to Black are particularly useful. You can combine several effects on a single clip.

Exporting your edited film:

Choose Save Movie File from the File Menu. Follow the instructions in the export wizard, according to the destination of your finished film. You can choose between My Computer, Recordable CD, E-mail, The Web and DV Camera.

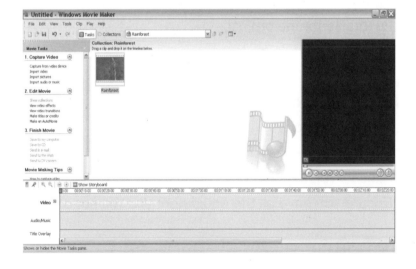

5.5 PRODUCING YOUR OWN ANIMATED FILM

PLANNING A PROJECT

There will be many creative and practical challenges involved in making even the simplest animated film with your class. You will work in a team and all contributions are important. With animation there are many different skills. If you find drawing very hard you could be an excellent model maker, a patient animator or an amazing sound artist. Give it all a go and see for yourself. The list below covers the main steps involved. Some are dependent on the style of production, and others on the time at your disposal.

The Mediabox website has an excellent set of guidance notes on producing and marketing a project:
http://www.media-box.co.uk/support/guidelines

THE STAGES OF PRE-PRODUCTION

- Create production team
- Agree on idea
- Fundraise for the project
- Prepare schedule for team
- Write script
- Create storyboard
- Design characters
- Make characters and sets
- Allocate roles on the production
- Ensure you have all the equipment you will need

PRODUCTION

- Set up equipment, lights and sets
- Shoot the film, following the script and storyboard
- Check all shots, rethink and reshoot as needed

- Record narration, dialogue and sound effects
- Compose and record music

POST-PRODUCTION

- Import animation files to your editing software
- Rough cut visuals
- Edit narration and dialogue to pictures
- Edit sound effects and music
- Add titles, graphics and end credits
- Master to tape and/or DVD
- Master a web-friendly version
- Design box art for your DVD

MARKETING AND DISTRIBUTION

- Plan and stage a launch screening
- Invite friends, relatives, VIPS
- Design a publicity poster
- Write a press release
- Publicize the film on local television, radio and in press
- Publish the film on the internet
- Send the film to festivals and television companies
- Get rich and famous!

FUNDING A PROJECT

Small projects should be easy to make in school without the need to raise money for additional resources. So long as you have the equipment and a time allocation within the curriculum, you are all set to begin. Many styles of animation can be made using day to day resources found in any art room and stationary cupboard.

However, you may be starting to get more ambitious, and want to make something which will really make a splash at a film festival.

There are several funding bodies you can apply to for help in the United Kingdom.

The leading organization which supports filmmaking by young people in the United Kingdom is First Light Movies. 'First Light Movies funds and inspires young people, throughout the UK, to make films reflecting the diversity of their lives.'

Visit their website at http://www.firstlightmovies.com/

Another good source of finance is The National Lottery funded Grants for the Arts scheme, administered by Arts Council England. http://www.artscouncil.org.uk/funding/grants-arts/

Other grant sources can be found via Funder Finder: http://www.funderfinder.org.uk/

Still from a cut-out animation

5.6 REFERENCE

BOOKS ON ANIMATION

The books listed below are only a representative sample. There are many books available about making animated films and there are also countless titles about animation culture and history.

Beck, J., *Animation Art: From Pencil to Pixel, the World of Cartoon, Anime and CGI,* Collins Design, 2004

BFI, *Into Animation* resource pack, Louise Spraggon, British Film Institute, 2003

BFI, *Moving Image in the Classroom*, British Film Institute, 2002

BFI, *Story Shorts*, British Film Institute, 2001

BFI (Series Editor: Vivienne Clark), *Teaching Music Video Series: Teaching Film and Media Studies*, Cromwell Press Ltd, 2005

BFI, *Teaching Music Videos*, Pete Fraser, British Film Institute, 2005

Blair, P., *Animation*, Walter Foster Publishing, 2007

Blair, P., *Cartooning: Discovering the Secrets of Character Design*, Walter Foster Publishing, 2006

Clarke, J., *The Virgin Film Guide: Animated Films*, Virgin Books, 2007

Cotton, B. and Oliver, R., *Understanding Hypermedia 2.00*, Phaidon, 1997

Furniss, M., *Art in Motion: Animation Aesthetics*, John Libbey Books, 2008

Laybourne, K., *The Animation Book*, Crown Books, 1999

Mealing, S., *The Art and Science of Computer Animation*, Intellect Books, 1997

Parker, P., *The Art and Science of Screenwriting*, Intellect Books, 1997

Patmore, C., *The Complete Animation Course*, Barrons Educational Services, 2003

Priebe, Ken A., *The Art of Stop-Motion Animation*, Delmar, 2006

Solomon, C., *The History of Animation–Enchanted Drawings*, Outlet Books, 1994

Taylor, R., *The Encyclopaedia of Animation Techniques*, Focal Press, 1999

Thomas, B., *Disney's Art of Animation*, Hyperion, 1997

Wells, P., *The Fundamentals of Animation, AVA Publishing SA*, 2006

Wells, P., *Understanding Animation*, Routledge, 1998

White, T., *The Animator's Workbook*, Phaidon, 1988

Williams, R., *The Animator's Survival Handbook*, Faber and Faber, 2002

RECOMMENDED ANIMATORS

Here's a selective list of work by a range of animators and animation studios which may help you think about approaches you can take in your filmmaking and viewing. We have chosen them as artists who we feel have defined a highly individual and distinctive approach to the medium. The examples are listed according to genre.

More examples can be found in **1.1 Animation History.**

Drawn animation:

Emile Cohl, Un Drame Chez les Fantoches, 1908
A classic pioneering work teamed with the generative music of Karlheinz Essl. Watch it here: http://vimeo.com/16274755

Otto Messmer, *Felix the Cat*, The Stone Age, 1922
Watch it here: http://www.dailymotion.com/video/xt4q1_felix-the-cat-master-cylinder_shortfilms

Chuck Jones, *Bugs Bunny,* 1930–1969
Watch a compilation of his legendary work here:
http://www.youtube.com/watch?v=kEKsaZNiRsE

Max Fleischer, Betty Boop: Minnie the Moocher, 1932
A classic Betty Boop cartoon with superb musical accompaniment from Cab Calloway and his orchestra. Watch it here:
http://video.google.com/videoplay?docid=2683613321391359141#

John Halas and Joy Bachelor, *Animal Farm*, 1954
Animation with a political theme. Watch it here:
http://stagevu.com/video/bksakizngzhg

George Dunning, *Yellow Submarine*, 1968

Yellow Submarine is an animated feature film based on the music
of The Beatles. Watch the trailer here:
http://www.youtube.com/watch?v=ODNVo1o7w8M

Bob Godfrey, *Roobarb and Custard*, 1974

Watch a short intro here: http://blip.tv/taymai-tv/roobarb-custard-
when-the-books-went-bye-bye-511703

Paul Driessen, *David*, 1977

A drawn animation inspired by students' drawings. Watch it here:
http://www.youtube.com/watch?v=FVCxHP_W_rw

Sheila Graber, *Mondrian*, 1978

Follows Mondrian's career set to Boogie Woogie, his
favourite music. Watch it here:
http://www.youtube.com/watch?v=i5kZL6_920g

Jimmy Murakami, *When The Wind Blows*, 1986

The film is based on Raymond Briggs' graphic novel of the same
name, about nuclear war. Watch it here:
http://www.dailymotion.com/video/x8ey7t_when-the-wind-blow-
part-1-full-movi_shortfilms

Joanna Quinn, *Girls Night Out*, 1987

Girls Night Out won 3 awards at the Annecy Film Festival.
Watch it here: http://www.youtube.com/watch?v=ficrLSm-dYk

Bill Plympton, 25 Ways to Quit Smoking, 1989

Watch it here: http://www.tudou.com/programs/view/yLpikmiFsTo/

Mark Baker, *The Village*, 1993

In a closed community fuelled by gossip and suspicion, one man
dares to be different . . . Oscar nominated precursor of the
legendary series *The Hill Farm*. Watch it here:
http://www.youtube.com/watch?v=YbTgrxilDMk

Sylvain Chomet, The Triplets of Belleville, 2004

When her grandson is kidnapped during the Tour de France,
Madame Souza and her beloved pooch Bruno team up with the
Belleville Sisters, an aged song-and-dance team from the days
of Fred Astaire, to rescue him. Watch the trailer here:
http://www.imdb.com/video/screenplay/vi4227531033/

3D CGI and 2D combined:

Michel Ocelot, *Azur and Asmar*, 2006
Watch the trailer here:
   http://www.youtube.com/watch?v=ZLlnb821K7g

Oil colour on glass:

Oskar Fischinger, *Motion Painting No 1,* 1942
Watch it here:
   http://www.tudou.com/programs/view/PvmbCzO1q48/

Sand animation:

Caroline Leaf, The Owl Who Married the Goose, 1974
Watch it here: http://www.youtube.com/watch?v=fusYZ7eIhps
Website here: http://www.carolineleaf.com/

Watercolour and ink:

Caroline Leaf, *The Street,* 1976
Watch it here: http://www.youtube.com/watch?v=PnLAhCGMkD0

Painting on film:

Harry Smith, *Early Abstractions,* 1946–1957
Groundbreaking experimental work.
Watch it here:
   http://www.youtube.com/watch?v=-wYJ51nSXRQ&feature=related

Model and cut-out animation:

Granny O'Grimm's Sleeping Beauty by Nicky Phelan, 2009
   Watch it here:
   http://www.youtube.com/watch?v=clDv1jJhoxY&feature=related

Puppet animation:

Kihachiro Kawamoto, *Dojoji*, 1976
Watch it here: http://www.dailymotion.com/video/x701aa_dojoji-
   kihachiro-kawamoto-1976_creation
Wikipedia:
   http://en.wikipedia.org/wiki/Kihachir%C5%8D_Kawamoto

Japanese anime

Satoshi Kon, *Millennium Actress*, 2000
Watch the trailer here:
http://www.youtube.com/watch?v=vpGrD5wUzKE

Hayao Miyazaki, *Spirited Away*, 2001
Watch the trailer here:
http://www.youtube.com/watch?v=6az9wGfeSgM

Polish animation

Jerzy Kucia, *Reflections*, 1979
Anthology of Polish Animated Film available on 2DVDs here:
http://www.amazon.co.uk/Anthology-polish-animated-Animation-
Animacja/dp/B002R0SVPM

Zbigniew Rybczynski, *Tango,* 1980
Wonderful, multi-award winning film involving complex travelling
mattes. Watch it here: http://vimeo.com/14953710

Pixilation

The Quay Brothers, *Street of Crocodiles*, 1986
Watch it here: http://www.myspace.com/video/vid/42716807

Pixilation, photocopy, experimental

David Anderson and Russel Hoban, Deadsy, 1989
Watch it here: http://www.youtube.com/watch?v=XXU0iHg1oC0

Shadow puppetry:

Peter Peake, *Humdrum*, 2000
http://www.atom.com/funny_videos/humdrum/

HANDOUT: ZOETROPE STRIP EXAMPLE

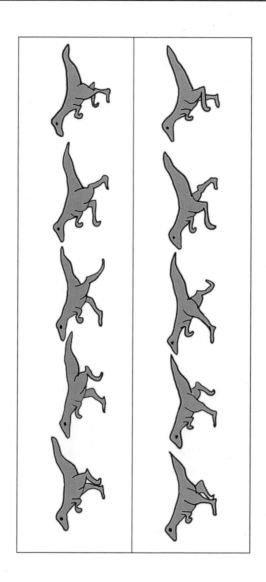

HANDOUT: TEDDY TEMPLATE

HANDOUT: STORYBOARD TEMPLATE

	SFX,Narration
Action	Length in secs.

	SFX,Narration
Action	Length in secs.

	SFX,Narration
Action	Length in secs.

	SFX,Narration
Action	Length in secs.

	SFX,Narration
Action	Length in secs.

	SFX,Narration
Action	Length in secs.

SPINDLE VIEWER TEMPLATE: 10 DRAWINGS

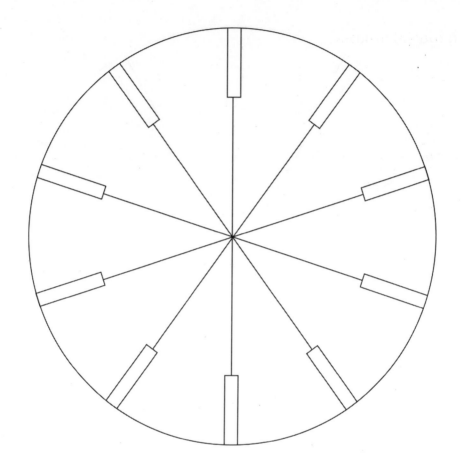

SPINDLE VIEWER TEMPLATE: 12 DRAWINGS

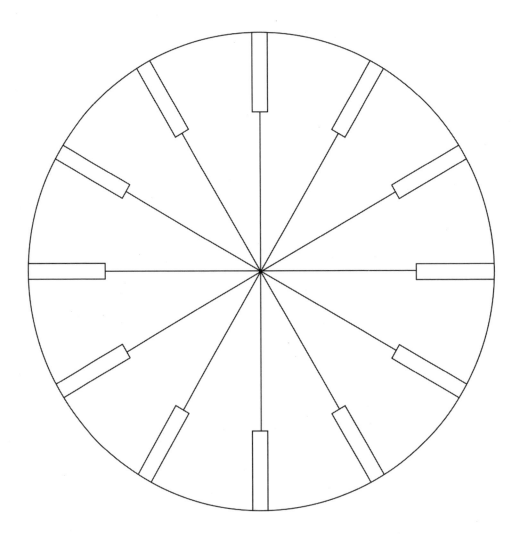

GLOSSARY OF TERMS

The following section lists a wide range of key terms and expressions that you will use, and want your students to use, in the creation of your projects and in viewing film examples.

Angle:

The angle at which you place the camera to emphasize an event, expression and interaction of characters. You can use high angles and low angles in extreme and more subtle ways. Watch the recently made *Peter and the Wolf* to get some useful examples of this technique.

Animation:

This is the process of creating movement to communicate the essence of an object or creature or situation. Animation transforms reality. Animation can more or less attempt to copy and mimic reality or to create something that departs from reality. Very good examples of animation mimicking reality are the films of the Disney studio such as *Bambi* and *The Lion King*. A more abstract example of animation would be a film such as *Neighbours*, directed by Norman McLaren. *Bambi* is a film for young people about a young deer growing up in a forest. *Neighbours* is an allegory for the human capacity for violence. *Bambi* is an example of hand-drawn / hand-painted animation. *Neighbours* is a live action film in which the human performers have been animated.

Broadcast:

Televised programming to people's homes. Broadcast TV has a long history of programming animation in various forms, ranging from *The Flintstones* to *Bagpuss* to *Wallace and Gromit* to the very recent *Peter and the Wolf*.

Budget:

This is a detailed overview of the cost of resources and hours in the creation of a project. The budget should be informed by the screenplay and story concept and in turn will influence the time frame available to create a project in. The budget, script and schedule are usefully filed together as they are all connected documents.

Cable:

Leads that connect kit to power sources and to one another. Cable is also the name of a kind of television channel that uses radio frequencies to transmit programmes via optical fibres rather than via over the air in the form of traditional television.

Camcorder:

A video capturing device, typically a mini DV camera into which a mini DV tape is placed to capture moving images and sound.

Censorship:

Censorship is a response to issues of taste and class and culture as to what is acceptable and unacceptable to screen for a given audience. *The British Board of Film Classification* offers very useful education days.

CGI:

Derived from animation but typically connected to visual effects: *Toy Story, Jurassic Park, Jumanji*, etc.

Channel:

A provider of a certain kind of programming on television. A channel can also be a term used to refer to a route taken by sound or picture capture into a camera or other recording device.

Cinema:

A venue in which to exhibit moving images. Cinema is also a term used to describe an aesthetic based around moving pictures with or without sound accompaniment.

Classification:

The process of determining the suitability of a film for its intended audience. *The British Board of Film Classification* is legally obliged to classify each film that is to be released in the United

Kingdom. U, PG, 12, 15 and 18 indicate the kind of film available. The *BBFC* has an education and information department.

Close-up:

A framing size that emphasizes a character (human or otherwise) in an intense way from the neck up. Close-ups tend to be used for the most powerful and important emotional moments of a film. Very good examples are to be seen in the *Wallace and Gromit* films and *Pixar*'s films.

Composer:

The composer creates pieces of music to accompany the images and sounds of a film. The composer typically works on the film once it has been edited together. Composers from the worlds of classical music, such as Dimitri Shostakovich, Aaron Copland and Ralph Vaughan Williams have written music for films. Music for films has also been written by musicians such as Peter Gabriel and Philip Glass. In animation specifically, one of the most famous pieces of music that has recently been used has been Sergei Prokofiev's music *Peter and the Wolf* which was recently used for the Suzie Templeton animated film adaptation. This way of putting animated characters to music is different to the way in which Norman McLaren, for example, creates animated, 'experimental' films, to music. There are infinite ways to create music to accompany an animated film.

Cut:

This is a command that can be stated during the making of a film in order to state the end of take. A cut also refers to the point where one frame joins another in the process editing. A cut can emphasize continuity or be far more 'unrealistic'. Sergei Eisenstein developed an idea of montage editing. Editing is not solely about eliminating material but recombining and composing it by cutting it together in a variety of ways—infinite ways—to create a range of emotional and intellectual effects.

Dialogue:

This is the spoken word that develops between characters. Dialogue is typically synchronous with characters' mouth movement though there are exceptions to the convention. Not all animated films require dialogue for their interest and meaning. When creating dialogue think of quite brief statements rather than longer statements or replies.

Digital:

This covers technology that records information as 1s and 0s. It is the opposite of analogue. Digital refers to the technology that has resulted in smaller, more affordable camera, sound and editing technologies. Digital can compress information to a degree whereby picture quality is higher. Digital has also allowed the editing process, on computer, to become very similar to word processing where files are managed and images can be readily copied, cut, pasted and rearranged. In this digital age perhaps it is more accurate to talk about digital movies rather than film.

Director:

The person responsible for making choices and decisions given to them from all those available in terms of resources and the crew they are working with. A director is not a dictator but is the ultimate gatekeeper of creative decisions.

DV:

Abbreviation for digital video: we can use DV tapes to record onto. We can also talk about a DV aesthetic: a certain kind of story and way of visualizing action that fits with low budget, minimum resources.

Editor:

The editor composes the films by piecing shots and sequences together and rearranging the shot and recorded material often substantially to create the desired effect. The aim of the successful edit of a project is to create a range of intellectual and emotional effects on the viewer so that they are entertained, informed and engaged. If time and resources allow you can edit your film alongside the production of it and this may allow you to see where you might need new or additional material created in order to tell the story as clearly as possible.

Fade:

The image gradually goes to black or any other colour of choice.

Feature:

Any film running over 60 minutes.

Film:

The material on which images can be recorded. Also the term we use to suggest the kind of narrative and aesthetic experience that tends to centre on characters experiencing dilemmas and emotional and intellectual problems that the audience is invited to relate to. We still use the word 'film' when referring to making projects using video.

Focus:

By focusing through an adjustment of the camera lens the filmmaker can control the degree to which the image you are showing is absolutely clear and sharp. It may be that you want an image to be out of focus initially and then to come into focus for a particular effect and reason.

Frame:

The frame is the border of an image. Framing refers to the composition of a shot, and what it includes. If you frame the image as a wide shot, for example, this indicates to your filmmaking colleagues that the image will contain a lot of varied information because we get some kind of 'overall' view of a setting and action and the characters in it. If you frame a shot as a close-up, your colleagues will know that the shot is about the detail of a face, an object, an event or a place.

Genre:

This is the term we use to define, identify and classify narrative films. Genres cross both live action and animated films. Genres are comprised of repeating character types, situations, motifs, themes and visual styles. Genre also embodies the values of a culture and can change over time. Genres fuse and mix with one another so that, for example, we have the romantic-comedy or the science fiction western. Genres are a quick and easy way to indicate to your audience the kind of story they will watch. If you say that it is a comedy people will have some idea of what to expect, for example. Live: occurring in real time, not recorded.

Key Frame:

The major points of movement in animation–see also Richard Williams' book *The Animator's Survival Handbook*.

Light Box:

A glass/Perspex-topped box with a powerful light source. Used by animators to trace artwork.

LipSync:

The matching of characters' mouth shapes and movement in time with recorded dialogue.

Live action:

This is the kind of film that audiences are most familiar with being built around the principles of photography that records staged events featuring human beings in 'real' locations. We think of live action as typically realistic.

Long shot:

This is the largest frame size available. The long shot (or wide shot) can be used to establish setting, time of day and a general idea of the action unfolding and where characters are in relation to one another. In the film Bambi the first shot is a very good example of a long shot being used to show you the forest in which the film is set. There are countless other useful examples.

Marketing:

This is the process of selling a film, of building an audience awareness of the film in terms of its genre and its characters. Marketing material (posters, trailers, interviews) makes excellent primary source material for encouraging pupils to think about how films are produced and how they fit into the wider culture and generate meaning and values.

Mid-shot:

A shot that provides us with more detailed information suggested by a long shot often. A mid-shot tends to frame characters from the waist up so that we can still see their surroundings but their expressions are becoming increasingly central to the action and emotion and idea of the film.

Mix:
The processes, after filming, when the range of sounds recorded for the film's soundtrack are combined with the right emphasis at the right moment in the film.

Pan:
When the camera moves, typically, fairly gently and with control, from left to right, right to left, either being fixed to a tripod or being handheld. A whip pan is a fast version of the pan.

Pixel(s):
Derived from PICture ELement: The smallest unit of a digital image, mainly square in shape, a pixel is one of a multitude of squares of coloured light that together form a photographic image.

Pre-Production:
The planning stage of a film: scripting, storyboarding, budgeting, scheduling, casting, gathering materials and crew etc. The more thorough this stage of the process the more successful your finished film project may be or, at the very least, will have the minimum of problems and concerns. As a word of comfort, filmmaking always involves compromise and problems do arise. Filmmaking is a human venture and therefore always open to imperfection. The lesson to be learned, perhaps, in how to deal as individuals and teams with these moments when things need to be fixed.

Profit:
When the money taken from audiences paying to see the film exceeds the production cost.

Programme:
A piece of content on TV, online: drama, documentary, news etc. Animation could handle any of these.

Projector:
The machine that a film or DVD is screened from onto a screen.

Promotion:
Promotion is another word we might use to cover the same ideas as the term marketing. It is about putting a film into the world and creating a set of specific associations with it. It also becomes an issue of branding. Think how we associate the name Disney with a certain kind of animated film or the name Aardman. The promotion of a given film is not only about promoting the film in itself but also, to some degree, the studio and producers who have made the film.

Propaganda:
This is the promotion of an ideological and political position. Film and propaganda have a longstanding relationship and animation has played a powerful part in this around the world. In America, Britain, Europe and Japan, among other nations, animation has been used to boost morale and promote messages and information.

Ratings:
This relates to classification. Most animated films that the majority of audiences will be familiar with will have a U or PG rating. This is not to say that an animated film cannot be rated for older, more mature audiences. Examples of this are *Alice* and *Street of Crocodiles*. These two films are not appropriate for younger pupils but may be deemed appropriate for 15- to 16-year-old students.

Realism:
Realism is the idea that the film we are watching is showing us something truthful and accurate about life—it's something that the audience recognizes based on their own experience of the world. Realism can be found in the way characters behave or speak and the kind of situations and subjects that you choose to make your film about.

Realistic:
We say that a film is realistic if it offers a view or recreation of the world that we recognize as somehow accurate not only in

terms of visual information but the way in which a story plays out and how characters relate to one another. Interestingly, we could say that Bambi is unrealistic because the animals in it talk. However, they also move with a certain fidelity to realism and their environment appears very true to what we know a forest to look like.

Recorded:
Videos record images; recording sound etc.

Registration:
Animation process, aligning each image.

Release:
The moment when a film is available to be viewed by an audience either at a cinema or equivalent or online.

Representation:
This is the way in which narratives in film and literature show the audience particular subjects in specific ways that relate to a range of issues and conditions in which a film has been made. For example, the way that women are represented in films from 50 years ago is different to how they are represented now.

Rotoscope:
A device that projects live-action, film, 1 frame at a time, onto a glass surface below. When drawing paper is placed over the glass the animator can trace off the live action images in order to get realistic movement.

Rotoscoping:
Rotoscoping is the act of filming live-action reference footage, for example of somebody walking along, and then tracing a drawn image over it which is then used as an 'animated' element. The use of rotoscoping in animation might be regarded as resulting in an image that is not authentically and fully animated but has instead been traced. Rotoscoping has been a part of animation production since the earliest days. The Fleischer Studio in New York city in the 1920s produced *Out of the Inkwell* series

using rotoscoping and the Disney studio used it occasionally in their production of *Snow White*. The most current version of rotoscoping is the form of cinema called performance capture, which is the technology that has been used for the production of films such as *The Polar Express* and *Beowulf*.

Script:

The script is the document that details the structure of a story for realization as a film. The script typically works out at a page per minute of screen time. Dialogue and action usually form the basis of a script. A script can be more or less detailed depending on the requirement. The script serves as the basis for the budget and schedule and these three documents should always work together when producing a project.

Script writer:

The person, or persons, responsible for taking a concept and developing into a detailed rendition of the story idea using dialogue and action. The scriptwriter might also be the producer and director but will often not be and so will work in collaboration with the producer and director to define their intentions.

Sequence:

A series of scenes that are unified by a common point. We could talk of the opening sequence of a film which establishes characters, settings, plot etc.

Short:

A short film, usually up to around 30 minutes, but typically 5 to 15 minutes. The term also suggests a certain kind of story and way of telling it. Animation and the short format have a strong history.

Shot:

A single uninterrupted take in a film; could be long, mid or close-up, static or moving, live action or animated, with or without human presence etc.

Showreel:

A collection of clips that showcase highpoints in a filmmaker or studio's work.

Sound effect:
A sound that matches an onscreen element. For example we see a horse galloping and we hear the sound of it galloping; we see a door slam shut and we hear it slam. Sound effects can also be used to contradict what we see or work in less logical ways. The animated film *Alice* and the films of Norman McLaren work well in this regard.

Stereotype:
A fixed, received idea of a person or event: relates to genre and realism.

Stop motion:
A major mode of animation typically taking specifically made models, but not necessarily, and moving them one frame at a time. Examples of this technique are: *Wallace and Gromit; The Nightmare Before Christmas; Alice.*

Storyboard:
A series of drawn panels that lay out the sequence of shots. Each image can be accompanied by written information about the scene and also details of scene number and any other pertinent information. The storyboard can be usefully filed with the script, schedule and budget.

Television:
The technology that receives signals showing programs. A television programme suggests a certain kind of content quite distinct from a feature film.

Timeline:
The timeline shows you when things happen. When editing, a timeline is a piece of information typically available to you in the software package that allows you to see when cuts in images occur and how sound and music run parallel with the images.
Ambient sound:
Sound recorded in the reality of the scene to give atmosphere: the sound of traffic for example.

Track:

Sound and image and also a camera move where the entire camera moves on a horizontal or vertical plane.

Trailer:

A piece of promotional material that condenses the tone, key story and character points of a longer work, used for promotional purposes.

Video:

To video an event is to record it using a camera that records images onto a video tape.

Zoom:

Changing the frame size in real time to capture a detail: we can talk of the camera lens zooming in or out.